EASTERN SENTIMENTS

Weatherhead Books on Asia

WEATHERHEAD EAST ASIAN INSTITUTE, COLUMBIA UNIVERSITY

EASTERN
Sentiments

YI T'AEJUN

Translated and with an introduction by

JANET POOLE

Columbia University Press **NEW YORK**

COLUMBIA UNIVERSITY PRESS
PUBLISHERS SINCE 1893
NEW YORK   CHICHESTER, WEST SUSSEX

This publication has been supported by the Richard W. Weatherhead
Publication Fund of the Weatherhead East Asian Institute, Columbia University.

Columbia University Press wishes to express its appreciation for support from
the Korea Literature Translation Institute toward the costs of publishing this volume.

Library of Congress Cataloging-in-Publication Data
Yi, T'ae-jun, 1904–
[Essays. English. Selections]
Eastern sentiments / Yi, T'ae-jun; translated and with an introduction by Janet Poole.
p. cm. — (Weatherhead books on Asia)
Includes bibliographical references.
Translated from the Korean.
ISBN 978-0-231-14944-0 (cloth: alk. paper) — ISBN 978-0-231-52053-9 (e-book)
I. Poole, Jane.   II. Title.   III. Series.

PL991.9.T3A2   2009
895.7'44—dc22   2009001580

Casebound editions of Columbia University Press books are
printed on permanent and durable acid-free paper.
Printed in the United States of America

c 10 9 8 7 6 5 4 3 2 1

References to Internet Web sites (URLs) were accurate at the time of writing.
Neither the author nor Columbia University Press is responsible for Web sites
that may have expired or changed since the book was prepared.

Contents

Translator's Acknowledgments

For their generous help with this project, I would like to thank Hwang Jongyon, Sam Perry, Moss Roberts, Vincent Shen, and, most especially, Suh Jiyoung. This translation was initially undertaken with the help of a translator's grant from the Korean Literature Translation Institute. A grant from the International Communication Foundation afforded me the time to further refine the manuscript. But still, this translation might not have reached any readers without support from Carol Gluck at the Weatherhead Institute and the dedication of Jennifer Crewe and all at Columbia University Press. I am extremely grateful, and I like to think that Yi T'aejun would be too.

EASTERN SENTIMENTS

Introduction

> In environments such as Korea, where one encounters a variety
> of difficulties when trying to handle the general situation either
> spatially or temporally, it is no exaggeration to say that the most
> partial and fragmented form of the short story has to be the most
> appropriate literary form.
>
> —YI T'AEJUN, "The Short Story and the Conte"

Eastern Sentiments is a collection of anecdotal essays and not short
stories, yet as essays the writings gathered here are, if anything,
more partial and fragmented than any short story, suggesting a
connection between their form and the environment of late colonial Korea. The anecdotal essay had been enjoying a surge in
popularity when Yi T'aejun was writing in the late 1930s, and his
collection is generally considered a masterpiece of the form. An
eclectic selection of thoughts on anything from fishing to stone
gardens to the melancholy of immigrant life, *Eastern Sentiments*
made fragmentation both its strength and its beauty. In so doing,
it offered the possibility of exploring Korea's past and present at
a time when fascism threatened the absorption of every Korean
into Japan's warmongering imperial regime. Yi's subtly phrased
explanation of the difficulties of representation under colonial rule
suggests a hesitancy to name the problem outright, perhaps due to
fear of upsetting a censor or perhaps simply because there was no
need to describe a situation of which his readers were all too inti-
mately aware. Under conditions of colonialism neither the spatial

expanse of the entire nation, that is, the geopolitical situation, nor
the temporal span from precolonial past through (possible post-)
colonial future could be freely represented, or, more important,
even known. As Declan Kiberd has stated simply and eloquently in
his history of modern Irish literature, "one of the objects of colonial policy was to maintain conditions in which the production of
serious works of literature describing a society in all its complexity
was well-nigh impossible."[1] The essay of the late 1930s has to be
understood, then, as a tactical and meaningful way to attempt the
representation of everyday life in late colonial Korea, when partial-
ity and fragmentation became modes for understanding historical experience.

Generic Revivals: The Anecdotal Essay

When Yi T'aejun wrote these essays throughout the late 1930s and
later gathered them together in 1941 into the collection translated
here, the traditional genre of the anecdotal essay (*sup'il*) was un-
dergoing a renaissance of sorts under the conditions of late colonialism. The essay genre had been popular among the Confucian gentlemen-scholars of the Chosŏn dynasty (1392–1910), who
would write down short anecdotes from their everyday lives that
exemplified their values and aesthetic concerns. Frequent topics
included the appreciation of poetry and nature, encounters with
people or even animals that allowed for the elaboration of a moral
world, and a constant concern with the ideal behavior of the gentleman himself. The language used was, for the most part, classical
Chinese, and literacy in that language and its canonical traditions
was an essential aspect of the identity of the gentleman as well
as his path, through the civil service examination, to a position in
government. That examination system had already been abolished
in the Kabo Reforms of 1894–1896, and by the 1930s a modern
publishing industry based in daily vernacular newspapers, popu-

lar monthly journals, anthologies, and individually authored books was flourishing on the back of rapidly rising literacy rates and a consumer culture emergent in the growing cities. The essayists of late colonial Korea may or may not have considered themselves Confucian gentlemen, but their essays appeared in the commercial print media and helped to establish their identity as writers of literature in a modern and professionalized sense.

As the decade of the 1930s wore on, the new essayists faced the growing contradictions and pressures of this flourishing, urban vernacular press and an increasingly harsh wartime regime of colonial assimilation by which that vernacular was repressed, to be replaced by the imperial language of Japanese. This most colonial of contradictions conditions the essay and other representational forms of late colonial Korea. Unlike their precedents, the essays of the 1930s were written mostly in Korean, but they still tended to depict topics of nature, books read, and daily life, albeit now a modern life in the city. The genre still granted great privilege to the cultivation of the self, but that self now increasingly resembled the sentimental and private bourgeois subject of consumption. Despite the appearance of continuity, therefore, there are important differences in the function, form, and content of the anecdotal essay that filled the pages of late colonial popular journals and newspapers, that appeared in individual author collections such as this one, and that was being included in the first modern anthologies, such as the *Collected Works of Korean Literature* of 1939, and thus entering the emergent canon as a minor genre of modern literature. Given this minor status, why might a popular and well-respected writer such as Yi T'aejun, who otherwise spent his time working on novels and short stories, devote so much attention to writing these essays? The fact that he was able to produce some of his best writing in this genre helps to explain his devotion, and then there is the additional factor of the essay's potential within the historical conditions of Yi's time.

The revival of the anecdotal essay coincided with widespread debate on generic form that was in essence a debate about literary representation under conditions of colonialism. The term *revival* might give the impression that the essay had completely disappeared at the turn of the twentieth century, which saw Korea undergo a harsh introduction into the global community of modern nations—as a battleground for both the Sino-Japanese (1894–1895) and Russo-Japanese (1904–1905) wars before becoming a formal colony of Japan in 1910. There was no period when the writing of such essays ceased completely, nevertheless, momentous changes in literary forms during the first two decades of colonial rule ensured that the essay of the 1930s sat among quite different kinds of writing than it had in Chosŏn Korea. After some years of experimentation with prose narrative forms, 1917 had seen the publication of Yi Kwangsu's *Mujŏng* (Heartless), which is generally considered to be the first modern novel written in the Korean language. From this point on the novel—understood along the lines of the nineteenth-century realist European novel—and, to a lesser degree, the short story rapidly became the hegemonic model for literature. The novel was so closely associated with Europe that it dominated models of literary modernity, with its heroes exemplifying the struggles of modern individuals in a changing national community. As in other colonized societies around the world, the novel assumed particular importance in nationalist circles because of its capacity for representing a broad spectrum of society that might adequately figure the nation and its progressive temporal structure, which allowed the depiction of the development of a society, usually embodied in the form of its hero, to a more heightened awareness of itself as a prospective independent nation. Thus the novel took on a greater significance than that of a mere literary form, ultimately figuring modernity itself.

In the mid-1930s, however, literary critics became concerned with what they considered to be the dire situation of the realistic novel. They were particularly distressed by what they considered its fragmented state, which according to them read more like a mosaic of disparate detail than a deliberate and organized narrative progression through time. Critics on the left especially lamented the lack of successful models of socialist realism in the wake of the collapse under suppression of the Communist Party. It was not only the novel that aroused concern. The fuzziness of genres now seemed to represent the lack of a definitive and obvious future for the anticolonial movement. In Korean writing critics perceived a strange mixture of genres: if the novel was too fragmented, short stories could hardly be distinguished from anecdotal essays, the anecdotal essay was itself in resurgence, and even the lyric poem was becoming prosaic. None of this conformed to the ideal modern order of literature as they thought it should be. It may be, however, that literary form actually conformed to the temporal rhythms of late colonial Korean society more than to the ideals cherished by critics and leaders of the socialist and nationalist movements.

The proliferation of shorter narrative forms can only partly be explained by the fact that such forms are more suitable for publication in the journals that dominated the field of literary publication. Yi T'aejun's own explanation points to the temporal possibilities imaginable in narrative within a colonized society. Conditions of colonialism prevented the writing of the epic realist novel, probably to a similar degree to which they created the desire among critics for such a novel. They seemed to favor shorter genres that took limited temporal possibilities as the very condition of their form. Korean writers thus confronted the same threat that literary realism faced in Ireland and other colonies, but just as Irish writers, such as Joyce and Yeats, found formal solutions to the colonial problem, so in Korea too self-expression could not be staunched. In reading beyond the realm of the canonical novel we thus discover the creative forms that responded to seemingly impossible conditions.

In Korea, the essay of the 1930s took on a different meaning precisely because it now existed alongside the novel. Its fragmented, partial form presented a different kind of temporality of the subject than that featured in the linearly oriented novel, which strove to depict the hero in development. Perhaps the essay could more closely track the artist in late colonial Korea, where the future of the nation was becoming increasingly hard to define in the face of violent assimilation and global war. The significance of the anecdotal essay as a colonial form, then, lies in its temporal parameters—its adherence to the repetitive presence of everyday life and its invocation of the past as tradition. These parameters, quite different from those of the forward-moving epic, suited the lives of Korea's rising bourgeois class—the class most implicated in the modernizing impulses of the capitalist revolution and that, perhaps, suffered most a sense of alienation from the cultural past. Two characteristics of the essay in particular seem to account for its popularity: its fundamentally ironic way of connecting past to present and the contradictory space it created for the difficult elaboration of a bourgeois subject in colonial society.

To take the question of the past first, in choosing to write in the traditional form of the anecdotal essay Yi was confronting a problem that was much larger than the individual self that features so strongly throughout *Eastern Sentiments*. This was the problem of how to understand the precolonial past as tradition in a society where that past had been appropriated and reinterpreted by the colonial regime. Such a dilemma distinguishes Yi's traditionalism from similar attempts elsewhere to rehabilitate the past at a time of rampant modernization and frenzied adaptation of all things considered new. For Yi to look back and see what had been lost necessitated an archeological project, so thoroughly had intellectuals in Korea espoused the new "Western" knowledge from the turn of the century, ignoring their own intellectual heritage. He faced, then, a problem of materials: there were few convenient histories or anthologies, oral narratives had been written down over the years thus effacing any possibility of a return to an "original," and many old texts had been lost and remained known by name only. This practical problem of sources was compounded by the colonial regime's own "discovery" of Korea's past. Such colonial knowledge—produced through the practices of archeological digs, studies of shamanism, government surveys of the countryside, among others—inevitably could not free itself from the viewpoint of colonial power. The past was in the process of being discovered and enumerated by forces with institutional resources far greater than the likes of Yi could muster: Korea had no university until 1924 when the Keijō Imperial University was founded and staffed by mainly Japanese professors catering to Japanese residents' children; and the first museums were likewise founded after the inauguration of colonial rule, on the impetus of Japanese scholars and collectors such as Yanagi Sōetsu. The question then arose of how the past was to be discovered, and this was for Yi a problem of form: how could the past be known and in what form could that knowledge be transmitted?

Yi's choice was to eschew the empirical and chronological narrative of linear history, which was itself a fairly new object of modern knowledge in Korea at that time. Gazing back over the past with a view to order and endow it with a master narrative leading to the present would mean to openly acknowledge that the past was over and that modern historiographical forms were superior for the understanding of its significance. Yi approached the past rather with the desire to relive it; he believed that it could be experienced once more in the present, at least in its better aspects. Thus the choice to write in a form that could itself be seen as a kind of repetition—of a classical form in a modern afterlife. With its traditional focus on the realm of everyday life, the anecdotal essay was ideal for an attempt to repeat the past, for it was surely only in the personal realm that such a project could be even broached by the 1930s, when the cityscape and professional spheres had been irrevocably transformed from their earlier shapes by urbanization and an encroaching commodity regime.

Of course, Yi's fundamental attitude toward the past was fraught with contradiction, and this is what makes reading his essays so fascinating. For if in their outer manifestation—the concern with orchids, with his garden, and with Chinese poetry—they share the concerns of a Confucian gentleman-scholar from the Chosŏn dynasty, their interior elaboration is profoundly modern. To start with, the basis for Yi's lifestyle is far removed from that of the old Confucian scholar. To take the example of the house that is the frequent subject of his essays: it was the redrawing of the city boundaries in 1934, in order to take account of the growing urban population, that sent real estate prices on the outskirts soaring and enabled those such as Yi to sell off partial plots of land to raise the funds to rebuild on what remained. Yi hired old-fashioned carpenters and set about building a house in the old style. As befits this modern act of restoration, his house is then filled with antiques, new household appliances, and bothersome or lovable neighbors.

How are we to understand the fundamentally ironic space of these essays? Yi was not against revealing the contradictions that formed the foundations of his project. We see an example of this when he approaches the question of the proper attitude to take toward the antique. The problem arises of where to locate the value of antiques. For Yi, the answer lies not in their appearance, or simply their age, but, as he writes, "in the traces they hold of having lived together with the people of the past." His fascination with the simple pot is enhanced by its nature as an object that mediates the relationship with the past especially well by dint of having once served a use in everyday life. All cracks and traces of dirt are deemed a virtue, in Yi's estimation, for their revelation of the past lives of people. More important, such objects recall a time when the relationship between objects and people was one of use and not mediated by exchange or consumerism. In other words, they recall a time prior to the commodity culture that is reshaping life in 1930s Seoul. Yet, what bothers Yi is not just the fact that objects have been appropriated as commodities but that, during the process, the old order they helped secure is being transformed. While Yi welcomes the surging popularity of antiques in his day, he laments the fact that not enough respect is accorded to the original life of the object. Plates once used to hold leftovers in the kitchen are now hung on the wall in the study, salt bowls become ashtrays, and powder cases now hold ink pads. The reappropriation of old objects to new uses is something with which we are all too familiar today, but for Yi it destroys the proper relationship between people and old things. What he proposes in its stead, however, is far from a "return" to an original relationship of unmediated use, if such a state could indeed ever have existed at all. According to Yi, it is the "proper modern interpretation as a work of art or craft" that will enable a new beauty and life to be infused into the antique, which will then enter contemporary daily life anew.

Something of what was involved in the reinterpretation of the antique as a work of art is suggested by Yi's essays on the nature of literature. He declares, at one point, that "the work is a flower that blooms from the individual alone." The modern act of interpretation enables the expression of the expansive self of the artist, which develops in relationship to the antique, preferably at hours of the day when the reality of social life can be best forgotten, such as in the depths of the night as family members sleep. He writes: "these pots may not catch the eye at first glance, but the eye never tires of looking at them, and so an attachment is formed. Once our troubled eyes or hearts reach there and find comfort in the absence of words, we begin to think of the distant past, which appears immense, but there is no sense of suffocation, only a pure heart remaining." The antique is elevated to the status of a work of art, which reflects back onto the artist a deep sense of self. At the same

time it presents a comfortable notion of the past and not the disso-
nant juxtapositions between old and new ever present on Yi's daily
walks through the city. This is a past that can be treasured while
colonial society strives to efface its traces. The contradiction arises
because this too is far from an unmediated relationship with the
old object, but rather a complex negotiation in a society now thoroughly absorbed into the colonial structures of the capitalist world
undertaken by an artist who lives his life within that structure. Yi
produces art for a living and yet longs for a time when art was supposedly free from such commercial contamination. Recourse to a
literary form that existed long prior to the new economic reality
might well prolong the fantasy of being an artist unimpinged by
that reality.

This dilemma of how to relate to the past thus helps construct
a division of social space in the present, whereby the realm of the
everyday life of the artist is, through its association with the past,
supposedly separated from the commercial space of the city. Such
a division—whether constituted, as here, through antiquarianism
or the personal essay or through ideas of domesticity and the private family—is not unique to the new bourgeois subjects of colonial Korea. Various separations of public and private characterized
bourgeois culture around the world, but the hard facts of colonial
rule marked the form of that spatialization irrevocably. Many historians of colonialism, such as Dipesh Chakrabarty and Partha
Chatterjee, have called attention to the way that colonial societies
tend to produce spaces of interiority that become associated with
the native culture against a "public" sphere controlled by the colo-
nizer. The idea is that within a delineated realm there is a freedom
from the colonial order; the irony is that very order produces the
desired space.

It was another master of the modernist essay writing about imperial society, Walter Benjamin, who perhaps most eloquently explained the relationship between such "inner sanctums" and outer

public spaces, stressing the inseparability of the two. They arise, he wrote, at the moment when "the private individual makes his entrance on the stage of history." For his purposes, this was the reign of Louis Philippe (r. 1830–1848), commonly understood as a time marked by the rise to power of the bourgeoisie and their domination of industry and finance. Rather than chronicle the ups and downs of their ascendance to power, Benjamin strove to account for the aesthetic parameters of everyday life and the material and technological environment within which this bourgeoisie fashioned their lives. He took as a figure for their rise to prominence the place of dwelling or interior, constituted for the first time in opposition to the workplace and derived from the fantasy of isolating one space from the dirty world of commerce and business. As Benjamin wrote:

> The private individual, who in the office has to deal with reality, needs the domestic interior to sustain him in his illusions. This necessity is all the more pressing since he has no intention of allowing his commercial considerations to impinge on social ones. In the formation of his private environment, both are kept out. From this arise the phantasmagorias of the interior—which, for the private man, represents the universe. In the interior, he brings together the far away and the long ago. His living room is a box in the theater of the world.[2]

By this understanding the interior is a kind of collection through which we can trace the fantastic illusions that sustained the bourgeois world. The organization of time and space—the far away and the long ago—around a box looking out onto the world is perhaps more frequently associated with a European bourgeoisie on the brink of imperial adventure, but we would be wrong to presume that the European bourgeoisie had a monopoly on the imagining of worlds.

Perhaps *Eastern Sentiments* is best understood as one such collection, curated by an intellectual from colonial Korea. Between its covers Yi gathered enough details to constitute his own private universe, his phantasmagorical interior. Great effort was required to sustain the illusion of the private individual in a colonized society where autonomy was in principle denied. Yet in reading through these essays we can glimpse some of the possibilities that animated bourgeois society in one part of the Japanese Empire and some of the impossibilities that structured its world. Just as elsewhere, the private individual was always a phantasmatic figure; in reading its universe in these pages we can trace the parameters of that phantasm in all its irony, with its contradictions, its obsessions, and its pleasures. In doing so, we have to keep in mind the options available to Yi for the structuring of his world. What kind of box in what kind of theater was offered him in late colonial Korea?

Late Colonial Korea and Yi T'aejun

Yi T'aejun and Walter Benjamin were contemporaries and, despite their ignorance of each other's existence and their distant locations in the capitals of Europe and a small colony of the Japanese Empire respectively, their writings reveal remarkable convergences. Not least of these is a distrust of the progress touted by those who celebrated modernity. In his final essay from 1940, "Theses on the Philosophy of History," Benjamin declared all documents of civilization to be documents of barbarity and accused historicism of recording the victories of the rulers and not the vanquished. In a short story written in 1941, Yi's alter ego protagonist glances over the books that line his shelves and laments the victims of the waves of thought that have crashed on Korea's shores in modern times. For Yi, being modern meant to have lived several lives and deaths as trend followed upon trend and the constant race to build a new order plunged people into instability.

To be sure, by 1940 Benjamin and Yi were not the only think-ers to consider the history of modern civilization to be a record of barbarity, but there is a special poignancy to such declarations by these two. Benjamin was the Jew stuck in occupied Europe, who famously swallowed poison when he thought he was about to be caught by the authorities as he tried to leave Europe through the Spanish border. Yi's homeland had been declared a formal colo-ny by Japan in 1910, when he was just six years old. By the time these essays appeared, the new order being so noisily proclaimed was that of wartime mobilization. In fact, when the new governor-general Minami Jirō had been appointed in 1936, he had announced a shift in colonial policy toward coercive assimilation, a shift that, as the war in China progressed and Pearl Harbour opened up a second front, was to turn eventually into the infamous total mo-bilization campaign. Over these years the language of school edu-cation would become exclusively Japanese, Koreans were all but forced to adopt Japanese names, and Korean-language newspapers and journals closed down in 1941, leaving only colonial newspapers and journals publishing in an increasingly distorted mixture of Ko-rean and Japanese. It was a catastrophic blow to the burgeoning publishing industry of the 1930s and those, such as Yi, who had emerged from its midst. Yi later wrote that at the time he felt an entire language was at risk of disappearing, and with it a people, whose fate he tied to language. That this moment should be ex-perienced by Yi as the end of the world is not surprising; he had a larger than usual investment in language. Other contemporary transformations included those Korean men drafted into the Japa-nese Imperial Army from the early 1940s, the laborers enticed to Japan to work in dangerous mines, or the women who were often tricked into sexual slavery for the Imperial Army or working in munitions factories both in Japan and on the peninsula. More than most, Benjamin and Yi were aware of the barbarous acts commit-ted in the name of civilization.

It seems appropriate that a form such as the essay, molded out of irony and contradiction, should flower in a society that was itself rife with contradiction and crisis. Late colonial Korea—by which is meant the period of the late 1930s and early 1940s—is sometimes called the dark period by Korean historians because of the policy of total mobilization instituted throughout the Japanese Empire as the war in China deepened and Pearl Harbor brought about the opening up of a second front. If this entailed a comprehensive policy of cultural assimilation that aimed to turn colonized peoples into imperial subjects willing to fight for the emperor, it also brought something of a rushed industrial revolution to Korea, which was rich in natural resources and ideally located for the production of war materiel between the metropole and the Manchurian front. The population of Korea's cities surged with migrants from the increasingly impoverished countryside, new factory workers, and even more military and civil personnel from Japan. By 1940 the population of Seoul had reached one million, of whom almost one third were Japanese.

With the rapid growth of the city, there developed a culture that fed off the gathering of new and diverse groups: resident Japanese, young Koreans away from their country homes and working in the factories or offices, and the desperate poor living off day jobs. Department stores, teahouses, a zoo, and other entertainment places were built and the new media—film, radio, newspapers—flourished. Over the course of the 1930s, newspaper sales tripled in part because of the rise in literacy as a wider range of Koreans began to attend school. The major papers began to publish cultural magazines that carried fiction, poetry, film reviews, and articles on society. As sales of these magazines in turn reached up to ten thousand each month, publishers started to differentiate their audiences through further magazines targeting women and children. The mid thirties are considered the first golden age for publishing; for the first time books could actually turn a profit or at least not

drag publishers into the degree of debt endured during the previous decade. Publishing thus took a commercial turn, where previously it had held the aura of a patriotic act undertaken by those
with money and education to devote to the nation. It was not until
the final years of the war that paper rationing and other restrictions
curtailed this emerging mass urban culture. At the beginning of
the war at least, wartime conditions hardly stemmed the burgeoning commercial ventures from earlier in the decade, and in fact the
new media of film, radio, newspapers, and even literature played
an active role in the total mobilization campaign.

Korea's first major bout of urbanism thus coincided with wartime production and a global age of fascist powers when modernist
ideology fueled art movements and armies alike. By the 1930s it
was clear to most Koreans that they had been fully incorporated
into the capitalist globe. Even before the vagaries of the Second
World War took off, the Depression of 1929 and its aftereffects on
the Korean peninsula merely highlighted the sense that events far
away would affect daily life in Seoul. This new sense of simultaneity
helped fuel one of the liveliest periods of experimentation among
writers and artists in Korea. Like metropolitan modernists, Korean
writers' interests ranged across the territory of urban cosmopoli-
tanism, transhistorical lyricism, and atavistic traditionalism. But
whereas the fascist modernisms of Europe seemed torn between
the future and the past—a futuristic celebration of the machine or
yearning for a preindustrial past—in Korea, as elsewhere in Asia,
it was nostalgia for the preindustrial rural community that so often
won out. For Korean artists this nostalgia was properly colonial in-
sofar as the preindustrial past was inevitably located before the age
of colonialism. The critique of the present was not only a critique
of industrial capitalism but of colonialism, or at least it could be
hard to separate out the two. There is no doubt, however, that the
late colonial imperial policy of cultural assimilation conveyed an
urgency to the traditionalist modernisms of Korea, bringing about

the paradox of a period of cultural assimilation that actually saw the publication of many of what today are celebrated as canonical works of literature, for example. This proliferation of cultural works seems to work against the prevailing view of colonial assimilation as the death of "culture." The politics of this culture are ambiguous, however, for just as the works of the 1930s celebrated a culturally Korean identity they often seemed to staunch any hopes for a political Korean subject.

Traditionalism in Korea was always caught between trying to recover a tradition more glorious than the abject present and trying to elaborate the past outside the imperial discourse that also appropriated it. A structural element of that discourse was Western colonialism and U.S. hegemony, which bolstered the idea of distinct realms of the West and the East, in which only the West could possess what it took to be truly modern. In this worldview Japan occupied a peculiar position as being of the East but yet successful in modernization and the appropriation of a supposedly Western culture. This idea was used to justify Japan's colonial ventures as bringing modernization to a "backward" Asia while successfully standing up on behalf of the East. With the promulgation of the Greater East Asia Co-Prosperity Sphere this appropriation of pan-Asianism reached its pinnacle. The sphere was justified as possessing a common culture and a common threat: Japan, China, and Korea were certainly not deemed indistinguishable, but their newly important particularities were supposed to contribute to a harmonious community. Newspapers and journals published reams of articles laying out the cultural particularities of Japan, China, and Korea and their harmonization into "Asia." When not found in the common threat of the West as earlier, common elements were sought in a shared past, meaning that traditionalism struggled to escape imperial pan-Asianism.

Yi's essays likewise constantly strive to read Korea's past within an East Asian framework—and a predominantly Confucian one.

Where some turned to shamanism and residual folk culture or Buddhist philosophies of resignation, Yi turned to the figure of the Confucian gentleman-scholar who had been so maligned by nationalists and Japanese colonialists alike for "failing" to bring about economic modernization and thus failing to resist annexation or being in need of some imperial "help" with modernization, depending on one's point of view. The *yangban* ruling class of the Chosŏn dynasty, who were supposed to disdain commerce and military activity while excelling at the poetry and arts that enabled their successful move into government, were now understood to be ineffectual and became an object of jokes in circles both Korean and Japanese. There is no doubt that the Confucian ideal of the gentleman-scholar—and it was always an ideal more than a reality—was at odds with the new citizens required by a capitalist society, and it is this, coupled with its not being of the West, that enabled the ideal vision to make a comeback in works such as these essays, where it took on new meaning as that which refuses the rhythms of the newly industrializing society. Yi's gentleman-scholar clearly disdains the modern capitalist world that is his home.

Yi himself had been born in 1904 into an impoverished but educated family. In the late nineteenth century his father had supported reforms and been sent into exile by conservatives as a result. He then died in exile. Yi was orphaned young but managed to educate himself, ending up at Jochi University in Japan in the late 1920s. Studying in Japan was a rite of passage for Korean intellectuals at this time, as was returning to Korea to find their skills unused in a society that failed to develop sufficient positions for educated Koreans. The figure of the intellectual who had returned from Japan only to save himself from starvation on the streets of Seoul by pawning his copies of Bukharin's *Historical Materialism* was prominent in fiction from the thirties, but Yi avoided this fate by lecturing at Ewha Girls' School and working as an editor at the newspapers. It was Yi who was chief editor of the arts section of the *Chosŏn chung'ang ilbo* newspaper when it published the avant-garde poetry of Yi Sang to such scandal and protest from readers that serialization was canceled. Only later recognized as a giant of Korean modernism, Yi Sang was to die at a tragically young age in 1936, an event mourned here in the essay "For Whom Do We Write?" Yi T'aejun supported many of colonial Korea's most experimental writers, but also began to publish his own work from the mid 1920s. Early in the following decade he was a founding member of the *Kuinhoe*, or Nine Man Society, an informal coterie that gathered in Seoul's cafes and launched a self-consciously modernist movement in the literary and visual arts. Yi was not a political radical and welcomed the decline in dominance of the Korean proletarian artists' association (known by the acronym KAPF), if not the political suppression that brought it about. Above all, he was committed to art and writing as technique and dissatisfied with what he considered the KAPF writers' emphasis on content and use of literature as a political instrument.

In 1939 Yi moved to the forefront of another cultural trend, which was the renaissance in the study of Korea's classical past. He was one of three editors—alongside his friend the modernist poet Chŏng Chiyong and *sijo* poet Yi Pyŏnggi—who started the journal *Munjang*. Although responsible for debuting many new young writers before its forced closure in 1941, *Munjang* had a decidedly classical bent from its very cover, which was designed by Yi's friend, the artist Kim Yongjun. The editors of *Munjang* consciously embraced traditionalism in an attempt to reconstitute and revalue an aestheticized Korean classical world—of art and literature—mindful of both the full-scale assimilation policy being increasingly enforced by the colonizers and the overwhelming advocacy of modernization at every level of society that had dominated the previous decades. Its pages included a series on "Korea's classics," which began with the first publication of *Hanjungnok*, an eighteenth-century princess's diary, translated into English as *The Memoirs of*

Lady Hyegyŏng.[3] It was Yi T'aejun himself who took charge of the serialization, writing an introduction where he extolled the elegant writing style practiced by court ladies in their diaries and letters.

In looking at Yi's traditionalist practices, we cannot help but notice a certain synchronicity with traditionalisms in Japan, and this raises the question of his location in relation to imperial discourse. Yi would certainly have been aware, for example, of contemporary attempts in Japan to establish court ladies' writing at the center of a new national literary tradition. Likewise he would have been aware of attempts to recover a nonsinocized writing tradition as the essence of a native Japanese culture. Some of Yi's writing on the female entertainers known as *kisaeng,* for example, takes him perilously close to ideas circulating in Japan that helped to buttress the notion of a unique Japanese cultural essence, ideas that in turn were conducive to the establishment of an imperial identity. But when Yi starts to write about the *kisaeng*'s role in upholding a native Korean tradition through the literary use of vernacular language, it is with an enormous sense of loss and with the belief in the past existence of something that is not, however, recoverable but evanescent. In the essay *"Kisaeng* and Poetry" we see that only a taste of the ancient vernacular can be discovered. The structure of feeling is then quite different from the articulation of a similar idea in Japan. Nor is there any doubt that those cultural practices that supported imperialism, whether wittingly or not, at the center of empire lacked the institutional resources to become as dangerous on the periphery.

Eastern Sentiments was clearly not considered provocative by the colonial authorities, having achieved the remarkable feat of being published in 1941 and reprinted twice in 1943 and 1944, at a time when wartime censorship and paper rationing was at its peak. Its Korean title is *Musŏrok,* meaning "Records written at random." The essays had been written over several years and published in various journals, but there is little that is random about their rearrangement as a collection at least. They move through various themes: nature and the transience of life, the Korean literary scene and literary history, contemporary society, and antique collecting and other traditionalist practices. The collection concludes with two travelogues: one of a visit to the seaside and one of a visit to a Korean immigrant village in Manchuria. It thus reflects the range of interests featured in the traditional anecdotal essay and gives us a fascinating glimpse into the everyday concerns of a writer in colonial Korea. By the time Yi gathered together the essays in 1941, he must have felt affirmed in his position as one of the period's most prolific, respected, and versatile writers. He had been serializing novels in the daily newspapers at a rate of approximately one each year since the late 1920s; he had published his first collection of short stories and was preparing a second comprised from the many stories that had already appeared in various journals; he had acquired sufficient authority as a writer to be serializing lectures on the techniques of writing, later to be published as *Munjang kanghwa* in 1940. He had the distinction of being one of the very few writers in colonial Korea who actually made a living from writing. But, as he browsed through the pages of his latest masterpiece, his satisfaction must have also been tinged with trepidation at the thought of what lay on the horizon. None could have been as aware as he, whose career depended upon the Korean language press and publishing industry, of the uncertainty that loomed.

Until this point, Yi's career had not been threatened by colonialism, but it had in many ways been shaped by it. With the increasing intensity of the war, the space that had been opened up for publishing was rapidly closed down. The Korean-language newspapers ceased publication in 1941, along with journals such as *Munjang*. The one official journal established in their place, *Kokumin bungaku*, published a mixture of works in the Korean and Japanese languages, but this increasingly turned to Japanese. Yi had made a passing attempt to comply with official prescriptions—including a rather bland report of a visit to an army training ground and attending the Greater East Asia Writers' Assembly in 1942—but writing in Japanese seemed to be a line he could not cross comfortably. A collection of his short stories did appear in Japanese in 1943, but it is not clear who was responsible for translating them. Finally, he moved down to the countryside until the end of the war where, he was later to write, he spent his days fishing.

Yi's intellectual trajectory resonates profoundly with the theory of the evolution of the colonial intellectual proposed by Frantz Fanon. According to Fanon, the native intellectual first proves that he has "assimilated the culture of the occupying power" before deciding "to remember what he is" by immersing himself in the culture of his people. This is when he studies history, wears native clothes, or begins to treasure local arts. Finally he moves into the "fighting phase" when he produces revolutionary literature.[4] Fanon was adamant that any attempt to prove one's nation's existence through its culture—as opposed to bringing the nation into being through fighting—could never prove subversive to colonial power. On the contrary, he argued, such attempts merely use the techniques of colonial power to annotate a culture that is far removed from the daily lives of the people. Such is the estrangement peculiar to the colonial intellectual, whose immersion in culture goes against both the current of history and the people and who behaves like a foreigner when he tries to return to that people by way of "cultural achievements." Some might argue that Yi did eventually move into Fanon's final stage with liberation. After the Japanese defeat, he chose to move to North Korea, taking up a central position in writers' organizations there and continuing to publish until he succumbed to the purges of the southern communists in the north in 1956. It is not clear what happened to him thereafter or when he died. Various reports place him working in a printing factory or even a brick factory. What is certain is that he could not continue to publish.

It is puzzling to many that the somewhat dilettante figure revealed in these pages would choose to move to the socialist society, but there are at least two factors that should stem our surprise. First, there was no more modernist society than North Korea in its opening years, bravely setting out to build a new national culture and pledging to remove the evils of commodification, which had so bothered Yi, along with all traces of the colonial regime. The work of art that Yi privileged above everything must have seemed better protected in this environment—removed from the vagaries of the market—than in the U.S.-occupied South where money ruled so brazenly. Then, there is the legacy of Japanese colonialism and the greater success of the North in promoting its anticolonial stance. Although Yi profited from Japanese rule, at the end it threatened everything that he had built up. He may not have been an anticolonial fighter in Fanon's sense, but he did live fully the contradictions of colonial society, and we can witness that in these pages.

The final image of *Eastern Sentiments* suggests that those contradictions find their base in the transforming meaning of the East. After hearing a child sing a song about tobacco in the three major languages of the Japanese Empire—Japanese, Chinese, and Korean—Yi walks solitarily across the Manchurian desert, where there is no horizon, no sound, not even a bird in the sky. The eternity of the moment suggests the disappearance of Korea is located in the diasporic displacement of empire. It becomes clear that the collection is at heart an elegy for a Korea that Yi thought was disappearing. We may criticize him for pessimism, but we must thank him for his loving adumbration of the object in all its detail.

Notes

1. Declan Kiberd, *Inventing Ireland: The Literature of the Modern Nation* (London: Vintage, 1996), 50.
2. Walter Benjamin, "Paris, the Capital of the Nineteenth Century," trans. Howard Eiland, *Selected Writings,* vol. 3, *1935–1938* (Cambridge: Belknap, 2002), 38.

3. *The Memoirs of Lady Hyegyŏng: The Autobiographical Writings of a Crown Princess of Eighteenth-Century Korea*, ed. and trans. JaHyun Kim Haboush (Berkeley: University of California Press, 1996).

4. Frantz Fanon, *The Wretched of the Earth*, trans. Constance Farrington (London: MacGibbon and Kee, 1965), 179–80.

Walls

Upon visiting someone's home, there is nothing I envy more than a room with a fine wall. Tall and wide, receiving only indirect sunlight, a wall as silent as if it were underwater . . . how calm it feels to sit alone before such a wall and gaze upon an old picture; to saunter beside a wall while pondering one's thoughts; to gaze upon that wall with several friends, partaking in conversation of no import as night stealthily falls; and sometimes to replace the picture with another. What support we can find in such a wall each day and throughout our lives!

Yesterday I visited K in S hospital. Three beds were spread out generously in the newly built second-class ward, and before them there rose a long wall. The light was indirect and a cream-colored paint made the wall appear soft and dim.

We all agreed it was a fine wall. And we all agreed that it was wasted. Not a single fly had paused to rest on this splendid wall.

All the walls were the same. Here there was a door and there a window, but otherwise these expansive walls were all empty, like a desert. The convalescing patients could run their weary eyes over and over this desert, but with nowhere to rest they would soon have to lower their eyelids.

I considered the thought that the walls of a prison must be like this. And then, for the sake of my painter friend K, I felt the urge to take my fountain pen and draw even just one line of ink on that desertlike wall.

I yearn for such walls.

I want to hang an old picture in a fading scroll on a broad, dim wall and sit quietly beneath it. The more our lives lose their aura, the more I seem to yearn for walls.

Water

I am watching the water.

As it flows by, the water is beautiful.

It seeps out from the earth and flows over the earth, but it is not dirty; it is as clear as when poured into a clean glass. It glides past the grass, raising ripples against the pebbles and happily singing as it flows beneath the blue sky.

The water is beautiful. The form and sound of its flow are beautiful, but even more beautiful is its pure virtue; it possesses that gentle virtue of not dirtying others and even cleanses them of their dirt. When we encounter water, how pure our hearts become; when we acquaint ourselves with water, how our bodies are cleansed!

One look at the water reveals that it harbors great joy. This is not only the joy of a song upon encountering rapids. There is also the great joy of an eternally unvoiced optimism. Instead of growing flustered when blocked by mountain after mountain, the water gathers and continues to gather quietly until it overflows another day. Whether poured into a jar or driven into narrow iron pipes underground, water still displays quiet forbearance and calm.

Water is sacred. It flows without interest; sea creatures live in its bosom, and rice paddies, fields, and orchards flourish because of its lack of worldly desire.

What creature does not benefit from the virtue of water?

Beautiful water, happy water, benevolent water . . . the sage Laozi wrote, "Perfect mastery works like water."*

---

* Laozi, *Dao de jing*, stanza 8.

Night

Whenever I returned from Tokyo to Korea, I experienced the night anew.

Of course day and night exist there too, but, having accustomed myself to the well-lit stations in Japan, I would discover night again once the train had left Pusan and began to stop from time to time in the most unlikely of dark places. I would look out, wondering if the train had broken down, only to glimpse station employees flitting back and forth like bats, and then a closer inspection would reveal the flicker of an oil lamp in the distance.

Night, the true dark night! It was not a copy but the real thing that I felt then. And in that dark, deserted village my heart would embrace the comfortable feeling of having returned home.

"Oh, what a desolate station . . . "

Some travelers must feel this way, but I was always thankful to find myself in such a dark station, after my nerves had been exhausted by life in the bright city and by my constantly passing through stations bedecked in lights. That feeling could only be surpassed by standing in front of some breathtaking scenery.

From that time on, I made a habit of enjoying the dark, unlit night. After I returned to Tokyo, I formed a group that met in unlit rooms; we friends would linger through the long night until day broke.

Although we see the night fall every day, still it takes us by surprise. And so sometimes I sit and wait from daylight hours. The night meanders in through the closed door. It removes my mother's face from a photograph hung on the wall, coils around a lone blossom on my desk, its eyes wide open to the very end, and then I find myself in the depth of the mountains.

There I encounter the cries of insects and wait for the dream that will surely visit; deep into the night I hear a cock crow in a village far away.

Early Ripening

A friend returned from the field with a pear he had picked for me, saying,

"Look, I found one already ripe."

I asked when he usually picked these pears, and he replied that it was only after the first frost. But, as he was walking along, he had found just one that had ripened early and fallen to the ground.

I took a bite, but it did not taste as good as it looked. It was tough, watery, and gave off a scent somehow lacking in purity.

As I tasted the salty water of this fruit that had ripened before its time, my thoughts turned by chance to those geniuses. Those who realize their talents early and die soon after.

Someone once said that when a genius dies early there should be no cause for sorrow. Within the span of such a short life the genius precociously reaches the predestined pinnacle of his natural talents and could achieve no more were he to live any longer. But, when a life should last at least seventy or eighty years, it is hard to believe it could be over at the age of twenty or thirty years.

I want to live a long life.

In order to write well, it is not enough to study, but necessary also to live long. I would like at least to live long enough to enjoy that wise and refined old age, which begins at the age of fifty, when we are supposed to know Heaven's will, and then stretches on through sixty, seventy, one hundred. Like a ripe crab apple that has passed through the deep autumn of life, I want to fully ripen on life itself.

"Life is full of joy!"

"Life is full of sorrow!"

These lines are commonly written by those geniuses of twenty or thirty. But how can we know true joy or sorrow without entering into the autumn of life, those seventh and eighth decades that we call old age?

I feel a sudden urge to live a long life.

Death

The day before yesterday was the most beautiful morning we have seen in Sŏngbuk-chŏng this spring. Azaleas and forsythias hung their smiling blossoms over every fence, apricot and cherry buds fattened themselves in preparation to bloom, and sparrows twittered among the forest of flowers as if they were the only ones to notice that the morning was so perfectly clear. And then, from a house across the other side of the stream, there arose a wild wail.

When I walked out my door this morning, a hearse stood in front of the house across the stream, which had been the source of the wailing. On this side of the stream several people stood in the road, watching the dead go on his way. I too stood among them for a while.

But my eyes were drawn less to the other side of the stream than to the audience around me. Looking on and thinking about death, those faces all had a shadow hanging over them, as if they stood beneath a black sheet of cloud. Among them was a man who at first glance looked so sick I had to wonder whether it was possible to survive such a condition.

Veins protruding like an animal's intestines, his hands clutched a walking stick as he struggled for breath despite standing still. He seemed almost to force his heavy eyes in the direction of the hearse. Stealthily, I watched him and thought to myself, "That's right . . . this must be a little too close to home for you." He must have sensed my eyes upon him, for he shot me a glance of disapproval, swiveled his stick, and shuffled away.

That glance was as sharp as a dagger. "So you think you're beyond this? You think you won't die?" He seemed to spur me toward disillusionment with life.

I had not walked far before a wail arose from beside the hearse. But on the road leading over the hill all I could hear were birds twittering brightly.

A human cry! How unpleasant compared to birdsong!

It is probably only humans who rush at death with such an ignoble uproar.

If only we could encounter death with more reverence.

Mountains

When I asked the child beneath the pine tree,
He replied, "The master has gone to gather herbs.
He must be somewhere in these hills,
But who knows where in these thick clouds."*

I did not understand this poem when I read it at the schoolhouse. But the more I grasp its meaning the finer it seems.

Mountains evoke sorrow.

In Kangwŏn Province there are many large mountains. When I was ten or eleven years old, several times I walked the seventy *li* path from the village of Yongdam in Ch'ŏlwŏn to a village known as Moshiul in Anhyŏp. It is a mountain path: after each mountain there is a river, and across the water awaits yet another mountain, and then once you have crossed the largest river, known as Tŏunae, you begin to climb the large Saesumok ridge, which is all of ten *li* up and ten *li* down. I have crossed that ridge several times on my own in the summer.

---

* Poem by Jia Dao (779–843).

In the thick of those luscious primeval forests, which cover the sky, even the birds, singing in their own private tongue, provoke sorrow in the traveler who has far to go; and, if he stops to rest, even a trickle of spring water, dropping down between the rocks, will sound like tears. Although I was still young, when I climbed up onto the ridges and looked out over the folds of mountains stretching dimly into the distance, or gazed down at the black waters rushing around a sunken cliff, I too was pierced by the sorrow of the traveler.

Mountains incite fear.

One evening in Wŏnsan I was woken by a commotion in the street and went outside to discover that a mountain was on fire.

The elders said it was some mountain in Kangwŏn Province, over one hundred *li* away, but a mountain ridge some tens of *li* long had turned into a snake of fire and was crawling along. It was an awesome spectacle; we could almost hear the sound of crackling flames swallowing up tree trunks as large as houses in their path. Like a terrifying dream.

But mountains were not only to be found in the highland. They were also on the plains and in the city. All those things that made me struggle, feel lonely or sad appeared as a kind of mountain before me.

The Flowerbed

Every morning and evening he would bring his grandchildren to water the plants and spread some fertilizer, but, despite the meticulous old man's great efforts, it seemed as if nothing could be done for the dying flowerbed.

The broad leaves of the hydrangea and plantain lilies, which had once trembled in such an appetizing fashion, were beginning to yellow and curl up as though burned in a fire.

"There shouldn't be any difference between rainwater and pipe water . . . "

The old man looked sad as he sauntered around the flowerbed after watering it each day.

Then the rain came. We had wished so hard for even just a shower, but the rain fell smoothly for four days or so, until all the flowerpots were full to the brim with pure rainwater.

After the rain had stopped, the old man walked up and down his flowerbed, muttering to himself over and over again.

"All it takes is rainwater . . . all the creatures on earth need the rain . . . "

Those leaves that had crackled like autumn leaves at a touch now revived as if by miracle. The yellow hydrangea leaves ripened to a dark green, and the buds, which had shriveled before even coming into bloom, now swelled up like blisters and opened out sensually. The old man looked upon everything with admiration and stroked each leaf as he walked past.

The old man has long enjoyed paintings and truly loves flowers. A close look at his garden reveals not a single tree that has been left untouched nor a single branch that has not received his care. For his pomegranate trees he bought wire, which he looped around the tree, cutting off some branches on the sides and in between and bending other branches until some of the trees were made up of four or even five distinct layers. He has tied up a rose to form an arched gate and applied some secret formula to the peach tree, whose fruit gently bump against one another even though it is a young plant no more than a foot high. From time to time he invites guests to come and view this inner garden. Everyone declares it a rare treasure.

Yet, although we are fortunate to have such a flowerbed in front of our room, I cannot help but feel sad that I have not once been able to congratulate the old man for his efforts.

To my eyes the strands of balsam, which are growing in strides in a shady corner without so much as a glance from the old man, are far more beautiful than those four- or five-layered pomegranates on which all his talents have been expended.

When I see those branches, overflowing with boundless life and stretching out to their heart's content, cut by scissors, tied to wire and twisted around each other like a wicker tray, I can only feel distress. They are deformed misshapen disasters; there are no other words to describe them.

The old man says they are like red flowers on a wicker tray, but our dull eyes feel uncomfortable when we look at them and we cannot take part in such fine appreciation.

Nature is a God. There is nothing, not even one nameless blade of grass, that has not been created by that God. Could any work of God be so poor or incomplete that it needs us humans to improve it? Such a thought would be foolish.

It is easy to destroy or deform nature, but we do not have the ability to create or remake it.

The Banana Plant

Last spring I bought a banana plant in the neighborhood. Before that I had been given two or three cuttings, but they had just been pulled off a main root, and I could not help but sigh each time I wondered when they would grow large enough to gaze up at from where I sit, or whether someone as tall as I would ever be able to stand in their shade. Finally, I went and bought the striking, tall banana plant that I had admired at my neighbor's house each time I passed.

It was already a fair size, but I spent all my spare time feeding it fresh cow's blood, as I heard that is the best fertilizer for bananas, as well as the water we had used to wash fish and the watered down dregs of ground sesame seeds. Last year it was the biggest banana plant in Sŏngbuk-dong, and this spring we took at least five shoots from it. Our plant has kept on growing with the same vigor throughout the summer, and now the tallest branches rise to more than twelve feet, soaring up beside the roof and hanging down from the blue, blue sky. All passersby look up and exclaim, "I've never seen such a large banana plant!" Sometimes I place my chair beneath those branches and soak up the atmosphere of the tropics.

Bananas always look good. Under the blazing sun their green and fragrant shade feels more refreshing than the water we use to wash our faces, and on rainy days, when all the other flowers seem tight-lipped and depressed, a banana can sprinkle raindrops all over the heart as one lies behind a bead window blind and listens to the faint sound of rainfall broken up by its leaves. Anyone who grows these plants awaits the rain with great anticipation, precisely to enjoy that refreshing feeling of being sprinkled with raindrops while keeping one's clothes dry.

The man from the house in front of ours came over early this morning and asked if he could take a look. We went outside. "Why don't you sell that big banana plant?"

"Sell it?"

"You should have sold it before now. Once it flowers like that, it's grown all it can. It'll be sure to die next year. That's happened to me many a time."

"But even if it dies, shouldn't I at least enjoy it as long as possible?"

"What, look at it for another two months at the most and then let it go? If you sell it now you can probably get five *wŏn* or more for a big one like that . . . bananas are selling at good prices this year. I met someone just recently who was looking for a big one. You should sell it quickly."

Of course, I should be grateful for him telling me this. If our plant is going to die anyway, he was saying, why not get at least five *wŏn* out of it?

But I was not easily persuaded.

"What's the good of selling something like that?"

"You'll get about five *wŏn* and then you can put up an awning so that the rain doesn't fall on your sliding doors."

He had been as irritated by my building a study without any awning as if it had been his own.

I had explained several times that if I put up an awning I would not be able to hear the rain falling on the leaves, but he seemed to think that pure nonsense.

This afternoon he stopped by again, smacking his lips. "I've found someone who'd like to buy that plant . . . "

Unlike in the tropics, here it probably is true that once a banana has bloomed it shrivels up, never to recover. But this plant had spent two summers with me in my yard—no, in front of my own room even—and was now blooming at the peak of its powers. What a glorious honor! So what if it dies after it has bloomed just once? At least there will be fat shoots working their way up!

Ask someone on his way to buy a cow that has been raised, worked, and sold in its old age, and he will say that it is the custom to eat such cows. Probably it is not particularly cold-hearted for someone to sell a banana plant, which is doomed to die anyway, for just five *wŏn*. But when I looked over at our banana, which was gently undulating in the wind, and then looked back into our neighbor's eyes, I felt tears rise to my eyes.

"I'll keep it. But could you come over and help me plant the offshoots a little deeper this autumn."

"What a waste."

He walked away smacking his lips.

Feet

One thing that struck me as I lay bed-bound on the floor was the strange appearance of healthy people's feet as they shuffled back and forth. Five heads, with neither eyes nor nose, stuck on the end of a body striding around . . . it was as if I had encountered some monster for the very first time.

"So those ugly things are people's feet!" I thought to myself.

Feet truly are the ugliest part of the human body. However good-looking people may be, their feet never rival their faces, nor their hands, chest, waist, or legs. There is no doubt about it; our feet were not created beautiful. When it comes to our feet, we cannot even compete with animals. One look at a dog reveals that his feet are much better looking than his face. In the case of the stone lions at Pulguk temple too, their feet are by far the most beautiful part of their bodies.

Not only are feet ugly but they receive the most abuse too.

My feet are the part of my body I use the most and yet take the least care of, and so it is with my wife as well. Consequently, the very first parts of our bodies to show their age are our feet. Veins protrude, wrinkles set in . . . feet age even before our hands.

But, then again, I think how grateful I should be to my feet! They may not be as indispensable as my eyes or my mouth, but they are always down there below, working hard to support everything else whether I am standing still or moving about.

We should feel many times more grateful to our feet than to our eyes or mouth. Sometimes they kick stones or are torn by thorns or stumps; whether entering cold water or grassy woods, it is our feet who must take the lead and risk being bitten first by snakes!

Compassion

It is as unpleasant as an insult to come across some poor child in the street who begs, "Can you spare a penny please?" It makes no difference whether I have no money on me or whether, unable to bear the situation, I pull out a coin. Each time this happens I am reminded of Shevyrev, the hero of the story by Artsybashev.*

. . . A landlady tries to evict a destitute family for not paying their rent, but a student, who lives in the room adjoining theirs and has seen this starving family trembling in their room for several days, cannot bear to stand by and watch and so pays their rent with the last of his money. He feels most satisfied that he has done a good deed and eagerly boasts of his action when another lodger, Shevyrev, returns home. Naturally, the student expects to be praised, but Shevyrev starts to berate him loudly instead.

"Do you think they are the only unhappy family in this world? They received some compassion by virtue of suffering in your sight, but what will you do about the countless poor people who are not in front of you?"

The student was lost for an answer . . .

At the beginning of this scene I was moved by the warmth of the student's compassion, but then I was overwhelmed by the much greater compassion of Shevyrev, who poured scorn on the student's paltry compassion.

This is not to say that my displeasure at throwing coins at beggar children arises from the same compassionate nature as that of Shevyrev. Rather it stems from my intolerance, which prevents me from reaching even the level of that student's feelings.

---

* The story is "Rabochii Shevyrev," published in 1909 and translated into English as "Sheviriof" in Michael Artzibashef, *Tales of the Revolution* (New York: B. W. Huebsch, 1917) by Percy Pinkerton.

Stones

The umbrella that sheltered me from the cold rain last night. When I came out this morning there were two small leaves, still wet, stuck on it.

They must have fallen from the date tree that I brushed by as I came through the gate.

I wondered why leaves would fall so easily, but then I noticed that these leaves were already spotted with yellow; they were autumn leaves!

Autumn! The morning was cold enough to make that wet umbrella feel like ice to hands that had just emerged from indoors.

I stepped down into the yard and stood before the flowerbed only to find that leaves had fallen here and there. All of a sudden the cherry tree looked gaunt, and patches of green undulated on the tips of the apricot tree whose thick branches were starkly revealed.

Even the flowerbed looked rather sparse to my eyes, probably on account of the fallen leaves. Almost every day I used to pull up a handful of weeds in different spots, but how tall and thin the flowerbed has grown during the few days I have neglected the task!

The faded flowers have collapsed, still clutching their seeds, as if the strength that had kept them steadily growing had vanished overnight, and now the sound of crying insects beneath their gaunt limbs makes me dizzy.

The asters and cosmos still have some life remaining. Their flowers will bloom gently alongside that autumn guest, the breeze. When I think that they too will not last long, the fate of autumn flowers seems tinged with sorrow from even before they bloom.

What is there to gaze upon at length?

However much I search the flowerbed, there is nowhere for my eyes to rest. Until I notice the clusters of stones piled up here and there.

Stones! I step back up onto the deck and look down upon the various stones, glistening wet with cold morning rain. I even feel a little ashamed that I have not become more attached to stone.

I recall those paintings of stone done in the Oriental style. Those Oriental gentlemen cherished the Chinese character for *stone* so much that often they used it in their noms de plume.

It was the heavy, calm, and eternal quality of stone that they admired. In fact, stone is one of those surprising discoveries of Oriental peoples. When we compare this to Westerners' obsession with the transient flesh, how much more admirable is the state of mind of those Oriental artists who painted and gazed upon stones and went so far as to incorporate stone into their own names!

Stones!

As I gaze upon those wet stones by chance this autumn morning, I yearn for the simple and honest state of mind of our ancestors who so loved stones.

The Sea

The sea!

Some people have never seen the sea.

When I was in the slash-and-burn mountain fields of Kapsan last summer, I asked an old man whether he had ever seen the sea, to which he replied that he had grown old without doing so. He said that almost all the people in that village would die without seeing the sea. A young boy at our side asked what the sea was. I told him it was a place where a large, in fact almost limitless, amount of water had gathered and met the sky. His eyes opened wide.

"*Pada!* . . . *Pada!*"

Quietly he closed his eyes. He seemed to be imagining the widest and largest thing in the world.

If I had never seen the sea, but just heard the word *pada*, what would I picture in my mind? What color would it be, how wide and what shape? And what kind of sound would it make? I am not sure what I would imagine, but it is an interesting thought. I cannot help but feel that there is something about the word *pada* that makes me naturally think of something large beyond limit.

The poet Chiyong once said that, of all the words for the sea, the Korean word *pada* was by far the best.* *Pada* suggests something much larger and wider than either *umi* [Japanese] or *sea*, because both syllables *pa* and *da* share the exclamatory sound "a," and thus, "aah!" I cannot but agree. *Umi* and *sea* do not suggest the entire sea so much as an island or a boat floating on the water, but when we say *pada* it resounds loudly, round and wide, as if we are summoning not only the sea but the sky above it as well.

Oh, *pada!*

We who call you by the finest name are the most courteous.

A look at a globe reveals there to be far more ocean than land. It would be more appropriate to use the word *water* rather than *earth*. Because people live on the land, they thought only of themselves when they came up with the name *earth*. If we had been fish, then it would have been called water, and the six continents would have been desert islands where the birds sing and flowers blossom and fall. Who would have built fortresses here? It would have been like the world in *The Tale of Pyŏljubu.*†

---

* Chŏng Chiyong (1902–1950) was one of Korea's earliest and finest modernist poets. He worked with Yi T'aejun in the modernist coterie *Kuinhoe* and on the literary journal *Munjang*.

† *The Tale of Pyŏljubu* is also known as *A Rabbit's Tale* and is the story version of the *p'ansori* "Song of the Water Palace." Composed sometime during the eighteenth century, it features a turtle sent by the dying Dragon King of the Southern Seas to acquire the liver of a rabbit, which was thought to be a miraculous medicine. The turtle has to trick the rabbit into coming back with him to the underwater palace.

August already! I miss the sound of the waves. And not only the sound of the waves but also the seagulls that chatter among themselves like young girls from another land and arouse tender feelings in me, the whistles from steamboats that float by like moving pipe organs, and those old friends I have not seen for so long.

"When did you arrive? How long will you stay? Would you like to take a walk?"

Their voices are all so much livelier than when I meet them on the train or in the office.

When evening falls, the sea also makes me feel sad. Many dreams surface when nights are full of the sound of waves. In the morning that same sound cuts short my dreams, and in the distance I hear the horns of weary steamboats.

The sea is the most remote thing we can sense with our naked eye. Above it clouds cluster and blossom like castles in paradise, and waves race along its surface like sleek, well-fed horses.

"Oh! How can I bear to stand still?"

Let us jump like flying fish, take off our shirts and wave them like flags. The beauty of the sand, reborn without a single footprint in its field of shimmering fine particles! Jump and jump again . . .

"Oh . . . !"

"Uh . . . !"

"Ah . . . !"

We can shout to our hearts' content without being ashamed of our hoarse voices, because our shouts will be buried by the sound of the waves.

Oh pada, you are as delightful as eternal Greece!

The City Wall

Each morning I step up to the inner yard, with toothpaste on my toothbrush, and turn around to find my eyes drawn toward the hill across the way. The clusters of the city wall follow the shape of the ridge, sometimes rising above it and sometimes falling short of it. With the high parts of the old city wall as its first target, the sunlight in Sŏngbuk-dong radiates out and down from the wall on the top of the hill. If you gaze up for a while, you can clearly see the gaps between each stone and the shadows cast by the pine trees hanging their branches down over the wall. As I brush my teeth, I often find myself surprised by the illusion that it is those stones that I am brushing. And then, when I look up again with my eyes freshly washed in cold water, I cannot help but feel that the wall looks more beautiful with the sun set behind it than in the morning light.

In the evening the wall is an unparalleled sight. Those weathered granite stones appear through the haze as if lost in smoke, while the evening sun, bending at its waist in order to shine, is no longer mere sunlight but a spotlight shining on an ancient work of art.

When it is still too early for dinner, I sometimes do not come straight home but walk up the hill to the crumbling wall and along the circular wall path at White Peak.

There are pine trees that have grown taller than my height from roots set deep in the wall. They must have grown from seeds blown here by the wind. In the past too, seeds must have been blown here, but the shoots would have been plucked out. These pine trees shooted after the wall ceased to function. A wall rooted in stone and covered in stone . . . stone after stone, as if counting grains of sand . . . when I think of the people who must have been mobilized back then in the same kinds of numbers, I cannot think of any other ancient artifact built on the strength of the entire people. As the saying goes, "A city wall is a multitude of people."

Dialects from all over the country, gathered from every place in this land, must have clamored on this hill, and the sound of chisels pounding stone and poles clashing must have been deafening to the ears.

If I strain my ears now, all I can hear is the sound of the wind blowing through the pines and the mountain birds singing; when I look up, only busy squirrels and clouds pass by; there is nothing else to see, whether standing or sitting on these crumbling stones.

In the distance, the evening sun falls on the tip of the wall and burns red like fire. Meandering along the ridge and burning at its upper edges, the wall is as awe-inspiring as a mountain fire I saw one night as a child. But it is only the evening sun, sinking momentarily. Watch quietly and nothing but the wind and clouds pass by. What is there but is yet nothing; if we think about it, this old city wall is not alone.

Autumn Flowers

I can hear the insects hitting the paper doors as they fly toward the light. Now that the rainy season is over, these past few days the paper has begun to stretch taut. When I find some time, I will be able to experience the joy of pasting on new paper.

When we were young we did not use plain paper. I remember pasting on the most transparent white paper we could find so that we could pick the leaves of China asters, chrysanthemums, and cockscomb and arrange them in flower shapes to one side of the deerskin-cord door handle. When the moon shone bright, our dreams on those long autumn nights were sometimes prompted by the sight of those dim red flowers.

The China aster blooms at the beginning of autumn, whereas the chrysanthemum withers as the season draws to a close.

Although they bloom and wither in succession, they both belong to autumn.

Autumn flowers . . . when other plants already bow their heads gloriously under the weight of golden fruit, these flowers prepare to unfurl their blooms on the hill out back, gazing upon heavy frost like girls whose wedding date is long overdue. Because of their sorrowful expressions, a quiet glance at them provokes sentiment even when they are still healthy.

The cosmos is more moving still. Perhaps because it is not an indigenous flower, it always seems to stretch out toward some distant place and bloom in yearning. When I stand before it, I want to write the sad romance of a faithful wife.

The China aster usually blooms in the yard and, because it is not tall, children like to pick it. It is not only on unbearably long nights that I remember how I would push that flower into a buttonhole or hold it in my mouth and shout, "Oh moon, oh moon."

Yet as I begin slowly to feel the weight of age, the chrysanthemum reveals itself to me anew. I do not like the tendency to refer to that Retired Gentleman of Jin at the mere mention of the chrysanthemum.* To turn something that is not an antique into a mere literary decoration is to deprive it of its dew-laden life.

I also do not like those exhibition chrysanthemums that have appeared of late, which bloom all too artificially, as if their heads had been permed. The old yellow chrysanthemums that grow around the sauce pots in the backyard or under the fence are finer by far. If they have to be planted in a pot, then far more natural and beautiful is the autumnal sight of a flower with a few sprouts sticking out, groomed by the clumsy hands of a gentleman-scholar.

---

* This refers to Tao Yuanming (365–427), who abandoned Jin court life to live in retirement for the last twenty-two years of his life. His poems of nature and drinking were a major influence on poetry of the Tang and Song dynasties.

The chrysanthemum is one of the four gentlemen.* We are grateful for the pure fragrance it emits after waiting for the cold autumn air and for its simple color, which can be painted in ink alone or at most with a drop of yellow dye shaken onto the paper to bring a flash of life to ink branches. It makes a fine decoration for a poor, rain-mottled study.

Even the autumn nights do not last long for the chrysanthemum. The water freezes without waiting for the flowers to wither. Place just one flower on the floor, close the shutters, and the whole room is transformed by the fragrance. We may not be able to embrace it, but to lie down with the chrysanthemum is one luxury belonging to an autumn night. It is even not bad if, just as I think we are alone, we are joined by a cricket crying in the flowerpot.

Autumn flowers know nothing of heat haze and birdsong. They bloom and fade under the cold moonlight and amidst the sound of old insects. That is their sorrow and their glory.

Dawn

At Pulguk temple we waited impatiently for the long summer day to draw to a close. This was partly because of the heat, but also because we wanted our first glance of the stone Buddha to be of Him rising out of the dawn rather than in daylight or at night. We had walked up T'oham Mountain in the dark and by the time we reached the Sŏkkuram hermitage midnight was fast approaching. From there it is a short distance to the stone grotto, but we suppressed our curiosity and spread out our pillows for the night.

---

* The plum, orchid, chrysanthemum, and bamboo are known as the "four gentlemen" in Chinese painting.

The silence of the mountain was austere, and we slept lightly, fearing we might miss the silent coming of the dawn. Our hearts throbbing with expectation, we rose even before the monks and waited for day to break.

That daybreak was an extraordinary event: a great birth for which we humans, like tiny grains of sand, could do no more than wait. As if fires had been lit on a fortress wall ten thousand *li* long, the rim of the Eastern Sea quietly drew a circle, and a light the color of the Milky Way began to radiate. We carefully climbed up to the grotto behind a monk. It was still shrouded in darkness. We stepped back in hesitation, awestruck. No one spoke. Finally, a misty phantom appeared above the thick, satinlike darkness: the color of the stone was soft, the shoulders, arms, and outstretched hand also soft yet solid; the smile was clearly knowing at every glance; and when at last the whole body basked in the dawn, it was as if He had just descended to this world and we could still hear the sound of His robes stirring as they settled into place.

The darkness slowly swirled away. Creases were drawn in the robes of the Bodhisattvas, cheeks and palms slowly emerged, and, on the slopes of the mountains in the distance before us, birds left their nests and took to the air. Mountain ridges were stacked up like fish bones. The Eastern Sea still sat enfolded in layers of cloud, and from their midst there rose like a single lotus blossom the Lord of the Dawn.

Loneliness

Ping!

Under the eaves the wooden fish strikes the brass bell from time to time.

That sound always seems so distant, even when it comes from nearby. It is not the only sound I hear. On the hill, in the garden, even indoors, the insects buzz like rain falling.

The sound of insects! Are they crying? But that sound is too pure to be a cry!

Whoosh . . . a breeze passes by. The brass bell rings out again.

I gaze at the lamp. It hurts my eyes. On nights like these, I wish it were an oil lamp that I might trim the wick and caress it like some sweet creature.

Just now three people are asleep by my side: my wife and our two children. I turn around to ascertain their presence and hear the sound of their breath rising.

My wife's breath is the loudest. One of the children I cannot even hear. Each makes a different sound. Their breath is as different as their shoes, now lined up outside on the stone step. Right now, that breath is walking them each through their own world, just like their separate footsteps. And so it is with their dreams too.

What did I sit down to do or think?

Should I wake my wife or my sleeping children? Would this loneliness subside if I were to do so?

Does the loneliness of life only strike when my wife and my children are not here? Does it not strike also when they are at my side but I am thinking of a friend? Or when I finally meet a friend for whom I have long yearned, only to find him a nuisance?

Meditating upon silence, in a mountain hall one quiet night,
Finding the foundation in the way things are, in forlorn
    solitude.*

How lonely this is!

And how inspiring of dread!

Yet, however great our fear, in the end, must we not all return to such forlorn solitude?

---

* This poem is by Yefu Daochuan, a Song dynasty monk renowned for his commentary on the Diamond Sutra.

Narcissus

I have returned home late several times during the past month because of work, some gathering or other, or simply because I was talking with friends in a tearoom as the night grew long.

Usually my wife and children were already asleep. The only sound to be heard was the wooden fish striking the brass bell with the breeze, but when I entered my room a narcissus, placed on my stationery cabinet, would greet me with a beaming smile, as if lifting up its heavy head on my account.

Narcissus.

"Where are you from?"

I whispered to it suddenly as I laid down last night. It seemed to answer earnestly in this way:

"My home is far away. It is not cold like here. The sky is the color of jade, warm sun rays fill the air like steamy breath, and water laps by, looking at us like a mirror. There are butterflies too. And even bees fly by."

It sounded so pitiful I felt my heart ache.

"You must want to return home as soon as possible?"

"Yes, yes. Really, I never thought that I would bloom in a room this cold where there are no birds to be heard and no blue sky to see."

"Do you want to see the sky?"

"Yes, the warm sky."

"Do you want to hear the birds?"

"Yes, and the sound of the water and the bees too . . . "

"Then why did you bloom in a room like this?"

"That is my fate. It is my sad fate to bloom wherever the water and temperature fit. That is why I cry alone each night."

This made me feel sad too.

I had spared it neither love nor devotion. I had believed that it was satisfied with my love alone.

As I turned out the light and laid down, I realized how cruel love can be.

But what can I do? Growing a narcissus is one of my greatest pleasures each winter. It is a happiness that I cannot give up.

How pitiful indeed!

History

If there were no yesterday, today would not feel this new. When we forget yesterday and are aware only of today, then we are no more than dumb animals. Of course, the fetters that restrain us because of yesterdays are large and heavy. Yet the path and ideals that yesterdays bequeath us form a beautiful spring, sometimes swelling to a river, that can flow brilliantly toward that faraway ocean of life.

When the way forward is blocked, looking back on the path that has brought us to this point can teach us as much as any textbook of ethics. In fact, the time has come when we must read and write a little more of our history. When Lu Xun urged youths to read more books from the West than from the East, it was because Western books tend to prompt readers to action a little more than those from the East. It was in order to push us Orientals into action, especially our youths. That is how it must be. However, I would prefer that we read our own books and our own history before those of the West. In general, biographies have formed the center of history, and hardly anyone who leaves behind some kind of historical record is lacking in dynamism. Of course, it is all the more powerful if what is portrayed is the life of a real person or an incident that took place in real society. The first lesson for the cultivation of youths must be history.

Not every document that records the past can be called history, and that is precisely the problem. The various kinds of jottings written down in idleness are no more than raw materials for the establishment of history. After everything has been gathered in the hands of a historian who sees with a penetrating historical eye and offers a convincing interpretation, only then can we call this history. History is not the discovery of a new document to which one adds a few technical terms in the name of "new research" so as to dance with joy out of the desire to publish.

Recently we keep hearing the words "historical fiction," a vague phrase that sometimes lures writers and historians into a maze. It is true that historical fiction means the fictionalization of historical figures, events, or objects, but the problem lies in the attitude toward that fictionalization. The heart of fiction lies, first of all, in characters rather than events. This is because these things called events belong to people. Therefore, what the writer seeks first of all in history is a character. Lecturing on history in the form of fiction does not constitute fiction. Neither is seeking out the private life of some person and writing an enjoyable biography. Fiction tries to excavate just one person and to grasp that person's character as painted in the documents. If it manages to understand that character fully, then it can animate everything that is possible and natural for that particular character, no matter whether it is in the documents or not, whether accurate or not. That is fiction, and that is why we term fiction "creation" unlike lectures or a biography. For the same historical figure, ten different writers will produce ten different works. Herein lie the infinite possibilities of art. As long as we stop at history or scholarship, we have to be tied to documents and limited to evidence. But the writer is a creator and, unlike the scholar, he has no obligation to his documents. Rather, it is not so much that he has no obligation, but that he does not trust documents. Historical scholarship means the ordering of documents, whereas fiction is the discovery of people. As a discovery, it will always bear the traces of the discoverer. Documents are far too lacking in concrete expression to provide the true reality of a person at a particular time. Moreover, with the exception of the *Annals of* *the Yi Dynasty*, there are mostly only irresponsible, impressionistic records. Documents about Hwang Chini too are of all different kinds.* They were all written out of their own interest, stimulated by words passed down long after her death by those who had never even seen her. Only an elementary student of history would recite such records arbitrarily in order to question the veracity of a certain novel. When it comes to art, we are eternal beginners. Just as the dedication to the pure way of film involves realizing that films are not mere illustrations of literature, the time has long passed for the novelist, and also the historian and reader, to appreciate that the job of fiction is not to interpret history.

Since historical fiction is fiction first of all, its critique is the responsibility of the literary critic and should not be handed over to the historian or scholar. Recently, there are those who brazenly wave red pens over historical fiction from the position of the historian or scholar. This is pure comedy.

History is the beautiful river of humankind. Do we not need a more accurate, concrete, and beautiful record?

For Whom Do We Write?

A few days ago we held a memorial service for our friends Kim Yujŏng and Yi Sang.† Considering their disdain for the secular world, we felt rather apologetic to be holding such a ritual, but we, the friends they left behind, were unable to cast off our ties to the

---

* Hwang Chini lived during the sixteenth century and is probably the most famous Korean *kisaeng* and poet. Yi had just finished writing a historical novel about her life in 1936.

† Kim Yujŏng (1908–1937) and Yi Sang (1910–1937) were two brilliant modernist writers who died of illness within a month of each other. They had both been members of the *Kuinhoe* along with Yi T'aejun.

mundane world. We would have been left with regrets had we not passed at least one evening in that fashion.

It must have been the saddest ritual in the history of our literary circles. It is painful enough to lose one person, but for two to leave at once, and both such precious people at that, leaves a wound that will not soon heal. They were dazzling athletes who raced alongside each other at the head of the pack: Yujŏng, who battled all kinds of difficulties along a path singular and true, as if it were his fate to write and to write in a style that was all his own from his very first work, and then Yi Sang, as brilliant as a mountain spirit with his wit and ambition.

Now that we have sent them on their way and only their works remain for us to enjoy, they can still inspire the hearts of we friends who walk the same path.

It must be said that our literature has grown remarkably during the past couple of years. Of just those works I have read, there is Yujŏng's "Spring, Spring," Yi Sang's "Wings" and "Ennui," Ch'oe Myŏngik's "Walking in the Rain," Kim Tongni's "Portrait of a Shaman," Yi Sŏnhŭi's "The Bill," and Chŏng Pisŏk's "The Village Shrine." All these are fine works of the like previously unseen. Even those that have a few rough edges are far better than the debut works of writers in the past. Newspaper novels may well remain another matter entirely, but if new writers continue to put out works such as these, soon established writers will not have the courage to hurriedly pick up a pen and write a short story, which is still the traditional arena for art. What a welcome development.

A place in literary circles has no owner. It belongs to whoever is writing great works. It is usual for new writers in the provinces to complain that they have no place at the center, but this is a cry of the weak. Kim Tongni shines in Kyŏngju, Ch'oe Myŏngik in Pyongyang, and Chŏng Pisŏk in North P'yŏngan Province. Artists are like stars: no matter where they appear they form part of the constellation. The only privilege of being at the center is being asked to write trivial pieces. Having to write many such pieces is rather an ill fortune. Just look from afar at how many writers are buried in trivial work and rotting away because they are located at the center.

But this is not what I want to write here. In looking at Yujŏng and Yi Sang and thinking of those other young writers, what I feel they have in common is their confidence. What does society demand of us? And the masses? Of course we must think about this. Someone like Yi Sang may look as if he never considered such things, yet it would be hasty to draw such a conclusion. Few have agonized over this point as much as Yi Sang. And yet he never became a slave to the masses. If Yi Sang had judged that it was in his nature for social consciousness to win over its opposite, then he probably would have written works of consciousness that sparked more fireworks than anyone else.

To know oneself first is always the wisest course. The work is a flower that blooms from the individual alone. The critic is often afraid in the face of public opinion, but for the writer it is irrelevant. Once he has judged himself accurately, then he must write in his own way with a clear conscience in the world. That I can see such a clear conscience in all the writers mentioned above is the greatest joy to me. The fewer readers in their sights the better; indeed, it would be no cause for sadness had they no readers in mind whatsoever. Such loneliness is the fate and the mission of the writer. To be alone, to suffer adversity, to perfect only the self given by nature, that is the glory of the artist alone, not to be experienced by the politician or the businessman.

In Maupassant's time too, it seems that interference from public opinion was severe for writers; witness the following, which he wrote at the head of one of his stories:

There are many kinds of readers. Therefore they make various demands.

Make me happy,

Make me sad,

Move me,

Make me fantasize,

Make me double over with laughter,

Send a shiver down my spine,

Make me think,

Console me.

Only the minority of readers will ask us to write whatever is beautiful in the form best fitting our nature.

Our artists must try to experiment with this last reader's demand, and the critic must analyze this attempt and appraise the result. The critic has no right to pick quarrels with ideological tendencies. He must not interfere with the need to write according to one's nature, whether that means lyricism or realism. If he does, he distorts the writer's nature to an impossible degree, stifles his creativity, and essentially denies the use of the very eyes and temperament nature has bequeathed him.*

These words of Maupassant set an example for us today. Of course we must raise our pens for the minority of readers that asks we "write whatever is beautiful in the form best fitting our nature." All other readers are mere idols, whether they number one or ten thousand. At first this may seem as if we are ignoring the masses, but it means neither to ignore nor to give preferential treatment. It is merely just. There are no words as simple for the masses to understand as "do it for the nation" or "do it for the masses." The majority can support such slogans, which thus exert absolute authority, like government rank. How difficult it is to proclaim to write for the minority! So many writers retreat in fear. Literature should always be

---

* This is from the preface to Maupassant's novel *Pierre et Jean* (1887).

literature, even if it is aimed at the masses. There are many people of no talent who write art like philosophy and call it thought, but with even a touch of the essence of literature all is transformed. Running may well be all the same, but there is a difference between running one hundred meters, one thousand meters, and a marathon. What would remain if I entered a marathon because it was popular, ignoring the fact that my body was more suited to the one hundred meters? Yujŏng and Yi Sang are people who ran in the category that suited their bodies. This is why there is a confidence to their work.

He who writes according to his nature reveals a creativity that surpasses common sense or any given concepts, but he who writes against his nature will produce no more than that. Religion is more superstition than ethics. Similarly, because it is art and not philosophy, we must demand that literature deal with emotion and not thought. Emotion is thought before there is even thought. Thought that has already become common sense and scholarly is philosophy and not literature.

The Critic

Recently the relationship between writers and critics seems to have become quite problematic, but in truth this is no great cause for worry. Notwithstanding personality clashes, is it not rather natural that they should oppose each other? No part of society pits individual against individual in the way that literary circles do. There are inevitably clashes between writers, and between critics too. Still more to be expected are clashes between the writer and the critic, who confront each other from their own respective positions. If both sides are sincere and offer each other due recognition, whether for a work or as a writer, then they will clash often. This by no means constitutes a scandal, either for the individual or for the literary circles, but rather should be considered an accomplishment.

The more criticism we receive, the better, either as writers or for individual works. No one wants to know the true value of a work more than the writer. If the critic's eye is fair, who would fear showing him one's work?

The critic who makes me feel uneasy is the one who fails to approach the work with a sense of endless possibility, but who instead tries to tidy it up using fixed concepts. This may be effective if the work has a certain logic, such as those by Tolstoy or many from France, but, for a modern literary critic, who knows that the more modern the work the less rational it may be, the stupidity of such schoolbook criticism is nothing less than a shirking of responsibility.

It is impossible for a writer not to have read the same theories as critics when learning about novels. Although it is natural to presume that a writer has done that much, there are some critics who jump in like composition teachers, as if to wonder where the writer could possibly have encountered such a methodology or theory. I would like to say the following to our writers. If you are lazy and ignorant enough to try to write, having learned about writing and methodology only from a critic, then you must give up any idea of being a writer immediately. Novels appear only through the deliberate avoidance of theory; this is because it is the nature of the work to disobey any known theory and because a work tends to fail in proportion to the degree to which it is representative of a particular theory. The birthing room of the work is, in principle, shrouded in secrecy. Even a newcomer will have written anything from one to some dozen practice pieces before producing that first work. These are people who have battled the myriad waves of a distant and deep sea where the beacon of theory does not reach. How can they not feel anger when the fruits of their hard labor are rashly set aside with the mere logic of those who have read the latest trends and methodologies in which they themselves are well-versed?

What writers wish is that the critic

1. has some experience of writing fiction,
2. is a gentleman who respects other views on life, a genius of sensibility rather than of theoretical concepts.

Eastern Sentiments

How many times has the moon entered the dark blue sky?
I put down my wine cup and wonder.

From people of old to people today, a flowing river.
They all look up at the bright moon; it has always been so.*

There is nothing but wine, the moon, and time passing like flowing water. It is that state of mind that has long been resigned to the fact that we cannot stay here forever and there is nothing to which we can form lasting attachments.

The myriad birds high in the sky have flown away;
A lone cloud floats leisurely by.

We look and neither of us grows tired,
That can only be the Jingting mountain.

The myriad birds and lone cloud all belong to nature; they make noise, fly about, and change. This is the state of mind that chooses, out of all nature, to declare its feelings to a mountain, which neither moves nor makes a sound. These two poems are impromptu verses

---

*   From the poem by Li Bai (701–762) titled "Holding a Glass and Speaking to the Moon."

by Li Bai, but it would be more appropriate to understand such everyday emotions as belonging to all Orientals rather than to the individual known as the Poet Immortal. Let us recall that the Persian poet Omar Khayyam wrote a similar verse in one of his quatrains:

"The longer we are in this world, the more we suffer. Those who depart early are lucky, and how happy must they be who are never born in the first place!"

Meditation is the genius of Orientals. Meditation was fundamentally ignorant of daily life but wise to fate. What emerged was pessimism. Seen from the point of view of reality, the way of the Buddha is a pessimistic religion. It is rare to find a high form of cultivation in the East that does not include the realm of Sŏn.* When the Europeans were in their rooms drawing beautiful naked women, were not the Orientals out in their gardens sketching strange stones? Such taste is not only restricted to art. The cultivated men of the East believed that poetry, calligraphy, and painting all belong to the same dimension. These men trained in all three skills; moreover, they were spiritual devotees of rocks in each of these skills. Thinking of naked bodies and imagining daily life, in other words, everything that is vulgar and inelegant, could not possibly constitute art for them.

Consequently, poets put their names to verse, which has long been considered the expression of elegance in the East, and their names were passed down through the ages, but the authors of those unofficial stories that are the expression of vulgarity could not even bring themselves to leave their names behind.

In this Orient, addicted to strange-shaped stones, Sŏn, and the pursuit of elegance, the cultivation of Western-style prose fiction might be a distant art ill-suited to the climate. Even in Japan, which

---

* Sŏn refers to a division of Buddhism that emphasizes meditation as the surest path to enlightenment. Known as Chan in Chinese and Zen in Japanese.

was first in the East to transplant Western-style prose, there has now been reflection upon what is "Japanese," and the "Japanese" thing that has been found as a result is called *sabi*, a phenomenon something like the patina of strange-shaped stones. It is one Eastern sentiment.

Stone is not sentient. How could people, as sentient beings, associate and even attempt to form affectionate ties with something insentient? Herein lies the hidden essence of Eastern sentiment.

When people talk of "the old age of stone" and crave longevity in stone, they mean something entirely different from the idea that "long life brings many humiliations." They are thinking of the Sŏn idea whereby the heart of purity is found in the eternal happiness of solitude and being of one mind. Just compare the works of Shakespeare and Dostoevsky to the old and solitary serenity of Oriental verse. See how much they have fallen into the world of gossip and scandal, full of clumps of flesh and the smell of blood.

Yet, victory lies with the Westerners in our modern age. However much we may look down upon them, the lament of the East lies in having to follow furtively in their wake.

The Short Story and the Conte

I once wrote the following in some journal:

"When describing life, we can draw a circle containing lines at many angles: the round whole is a novel; what is less than the whole is a novella; just one slice is a short story; and a fraction of an angle with no surface can be called a conte."

To state the obvious, the characters for "long," "medium," "short," and "palm of the hand" [as used in the words for novel, novella, short story, and conte respectively] refer first of all to the length of a work. Of course qualitative factors come into question too when defining the novel and short story, but with the short story even quality cannot avoid the fate of having to mature into fruition in less space than a novel. It is the same with the short story and the conte.

The short story arose as an economical form for describing life. That is why it is a product of modernity and not ancient times. When searching for its origins, there are many people who go way back to the Bible and cite the story of the Prodigal Son, but that was a mere happenstance. It was not until Edgar Allan Poe (1809–1849) that the form appeared as a result of self-conscious planning.

More than any other writer, Poe grew tired of reading and writing novels. Life does not only have to be expressed at length and in a drawn-out fashion; it can be enough to show just one side of life.

This, Poe's declaration on the short story, was received enthusiastically around the world, and subsequently famous short story writers appeared, the likes of Maupassant and Chekhov. As a result, innumerable attempts to define or prescribe the form have been essayed by writers and critics.

But there is nothing complicated about it.

Of all fictional forms, the short story is the one that expresses characters in the most economical and brief way. That is all there is to it.

"The short story promises not to treat characters, action, and background all as equals, but to achieve singular results by either emphasizing character or action or by stressing the background."

It guides the plot in only one direction by stressing one point and economizes on time and space as much as possible. It reveals to the reader an aspect of human life as emphasized in a short period of time.

This became necessary for both readers and editors, who with the inundation of periodical publications from the late nineteenth century needed many more short stories than long novels. But it was in the twentieth century that the short story truly entered its golden age. If we consider our own literary circles today, novels come nowhere close to short stories in terms of quantity, and, to be sure, in quality, too, novels lag way behind. Since our novels are mostly serialized in newspapers, they have developed under special conditions that differ from those of the original novel, and in their current situation, with the exception of so-called nonserialized novels, in every aspect beginning from the writer's attitude they cannot be considered true literary creations. Therefore, if we want to consider a writer's art and not his job, that still cannot be found apart from the short story.

To the degree that this holds true, it is no exaggeration to say that in Korea today the short story represents the art of all writers and, consequently, Korean literature itself.

Moreover, in environments such as Korea where one encounters a variety of difficulties when trying to handle the general situation either spatially or temporally, it is no exaggeration to say that the most partial and fragmented form of the short story has to be the most appropriate literary form.

Just as the short story came after the novel, the conte followed the short story. We could say that the short story results from the ennui of the novel, and the conte results from the ennui of the short story. No people in the past have lived lives as busy and as structured by time as we moderns. Some magazines even add beneath the title of a story a note on how many minutes are required to read it. In our modern lives, we need works that can be read all the way through while taking the streetcar from Chongno to Kyŏngsŏng Station.

Because of this, with the conte length is of more importance than quality. It is only to be expected that the preoccupation with a limited length has given birth to a most particular quality as well. As it is above all else short, the conte was translated as "palm-of-the-hand story."

The conte does not relate even one aspect of life. Unlike the short story, it provides an impression of an angle or mere glance at life. It concentrates all its power on recording in sharp detail the most focused flash of an impression. That is why the conte can be the meanest of technologies and has the tendency in its content to lean toward strange surprises. Such are the works of the American writer O'Henry. Bizarre observations and ideas and wit, nothing more. They really are sufficient for reading on the streetcar. They are a mere convenience, like a lunchbox to be eaten in the car and forgotten.

For a while I was fairly attracted as a reader to contes. I even tried writing several. They included "The Angels' Wrath," "Catfish," "The Horse-Driver and the Professor," and "The Banquet." Even now, when I recall my mood as I was writing them, I think, "I did not write them so much as make them" or, even, "I did not make them so much as put them together."

It feels like a kind of handicraft. And that is why I feel that writing contes cannot amount to a true and prudent life for a writer. Contes are nothing more than a kind of impromptu piece of writing requested from writers, as if many different names needed to be lined up on a few pages; they are rather like the rough sketches of artists that appear on the special edition pages of newspapers.

If there is any more value to the conte than this, it is as simple practice material for beginners, as a shorter version of the short story. As a whole, the conte is like a small glass bottle; everything inside can be seen clearly at a glance. Even the simplest eyes can quickly see what was the basis for the author's inspiration, the premise for the story's development, the way in which everything leads toward emphasizing one point, and how the narrowness of scale emphasizes everything to the extreme. Reading contes is the best way to begin the study of fiction writing and therefore it is also a good way to learn how to write, as there is less likelihood of straying from the subject.

This is all I can say: contes are not the true way of fiction. Just as newspaper novels show a peculiar development outside the true way, because they are too sensitive to the nature of the times, the conte is a kind of outsider in the realm of the short story and, even in the smallest of ways, perpetuates its own special position because of its nature, which curries favor with the world of journalism. Thus I do not think we can expect any more of the conte as prose literature. Prose literature is not just a vessel for one emotion or one thought, but a vessel for the whole of life itself. As even short stories can be stifling, perhaps the conte should belong not to fiction but to the category of the essay or witticism.

Titles and Other Matters

Titles

One of the joys of fatherhood is coming up with two possible names upon discovering that your wife is pregnant and still not knowing whether it is a boy or a girl. It is exactly the same with creative works. A title comes to mind even before the ideas have been organized, and, in fact, deciding upon the title helps to draw a silhouette around that boundless world of ideas. There is a particular joy in writing the title at the top of a blank piece of manuscript paper when it is nothing other than a wonderful picture. Even if I change it later, I usually start by writing the title. There are no real standards for deciding upon a title. For the conte it should be lighthearted, for the serial novel it should be fresh, a little showy, and sound good spoken out loud. But all this seems too natural to be any kind of standard. For the short story, however, the title should be faithful and represent the contents with honesty.

Structure

Before heroic tales of the ilk of the *Tale of the Three Kingdoms*, it is hard to find anything in Oriental novels that bears resemblance to the solid design, like that of tall buildings, found in the West. The form of life in the West is dynamic where we are static, and where they are solid we are flat. If a character is anywhere near decent, he will not demand a duel, go horseracing, or play golf, as they do, but will rather lie down in a pavilion to ponder, go fishing, or play *go*. Whenever someone tries to force change on such quiet characters and lifestyles, it usually ends up looking like the capriciousness of the author. Why are there so many *sasosŏl*?* There is something lacking when we make pronouncements such as "this is a result of our writers' lack of vitality." It is like searching for a sense of solidity in Oriental paintings. Structure . . . this is the greatest challenge faced by Oriental writers.

Characters

I used to think that as I was creating my characters I could do anything I liked with them, but this ended in failure several times. Once a face has been drawn, a way of speaking emerged, and a character decided upon, then even the greatest writer can choose only one of two paths—to be dragged along by that character or to take charge of that character. It is not unusual for a character to refuse to listen when the development of an incident necessitates a certain action. Even if it means the incident cannot be completed, there is nothing to be done with that character. Surely the luxury of

---

* *Sasosŏl* refers to stories presumed to portray the author's own life in fictional form. The characters mean literally "I-novel" and are more commonly known by their Japanese pronunciation of *shishōsetsu*. From the 1920s, critics and writers in Japan debated the *shishōsetsu* frequently, understanding it alternatively as a failed imitation or unique appropriation of the Western novel. In Korea the form proliferated during the late colonial period, where it served to demarcate the realm of everyday life within colonial society. Many of Yi's short stories from the late colonial period conform to the expectations of this form.

time to plan ahead in one's mind is the best way to meet the character who will carry through all the action that the writer envisages.

Ideology

Emotion trumps ideology in the work of art. Or, rather, emotion that has passed through thought or ideology that has not yet been sealed in writing as ideology. Usually the stiffness of a work stems from the insertion of an ideology that is too commonsensical. Therefore, the more ideological the writer, the greater chance the novel becomes too logical. However great the writer, such works end up as mere illustrations of philosophy and will not enter the VIP room of literature.

Material

I have a notebook on my desk, one in my bag, and another in my pocket, which means three or four in all. Whether I am on the streetcar or in the street, I write down everything that could be a word in a novel, a phrase, or part of an incident. If a photograph shows a scene or a character that could appear in a story, then I cut it out and keep it. I often use this directly for material and not just for reference. I tend to work harder at writing characters than events and I have used several characters that I found in photographs. The most distressing aspect of material, and I am sure this is not my experience alone, is that the more cleverness and effort goes into the handling of it the more we end up hoping to learn from our mistakes.

Sentences

Rather than writing "my sentences," I want as much as possible to write "the work's sentences." Most of all, I try to write "that scene's sentences."

Rewriting

I am sorry that I cannot make writing fiction my full-time job. I do not have enough time to rewrite my works. Of course, I cannot blame this solely on time, but have to admit it is a problem with my character as well. I am not trying to evade responsibility by saying that I have no time.

If the entire Korean literary circles could spend three years rewriting what we have already written, then we would produce works of far higher quality than those produced in three years of mere writing.

Korea's Fiction

At present, various kinds of fiction are being read in Korea. There is the old-style fiction, which does not carry an author's name and is usually divided again into old novels and new novels, and then there is contemporary fiction, which the author publishes as a literary act and under a signature of responsibility. This latter, too, is divided once more into the novel, the short story, the novella, and the conte. The novel is divided further into the serial novel, which comprises by far the majority and differs in nature from the original novel because of the particular form of its publication in installments in the newspaper, and then the "nonserialized novel," which refers to the original novel and has recently acquired this name in opposition to the serial novel. Clearly the historical novel is also another kind of novel.

First of all, I would like to say something general about the old-style fiction, namely, that it has not been accepted as literature in our current literary circles and the reasons for that. Within the history of fiction it is the fate of these old novels not to be accorded the treatment of literature and art, because their method relies upon the fantasy of divine help and they make it their business to praise good and punish evil and to celebrate loyalty and filiality in order to show that rewards come only after suffering and that all things will return to their true state. This fate is shared by the new novels from the time of Yi Injik, who began to write about real figures and real life in that period.* Works such as "The Tale of Changhwa and Hongnyŏn," "The Tale of Hŭngbu," and "The Tale of Ch'unhyang" are being reappreciated as our classical literature, but they lag far behind our current notion of the novel. This is basically due to the lack of sincerity in their expression. In fact, it is hard to find even one character described with sincerity. Whether we think of Changhwa's stepmother Lady Hŏ, of Hŭngbu's older brother Nolbu, of Ch'unhyang or of Yi Toryŏng, not one of them is properly depicted. From beginning to end their sentences are submerged in the traditional rules, which try to captivate the foolish masses with useless exaggerations and retorts for the sake of the pretense of knowledge and a good rhythm when read out loud. To give some examples:

"as Hŏ was to be married, her features surely had to be debated: those two cheeks that exceeded a foot in size, brass bells for eyes, a nose like an unglazed earthenware bottle, catfishlike lips and pig's hair; she was as tall as a totem pole and had a voice like a wolf,

---

* In 1906 Yi Injik (1862–1916) published "Tears of Blood," a story set during the Sino-Japanese War of 1894–1895. The story is known in Korea as a "new novel" that attempted an explicit reform of written language and, as Yi T'aejun suggests, refocused fictional content onto the present and a historically specific location.

her waist stretched a full two arm-spans, and then there was her deformed arm, swollen legs, torn lips, and a mouth that, were it to be cut and stretched out, would make ten bowls and was as twisted as a straw mat used for spreading beans; in fact, it was quite hard to look her straight in the face . . . "

This is the description of Lady Hŏ in "The Tale of Changhwa and Hongnyŏn." As a form of expression, fundamentally it does not take the "truth" into consideration.

"Ch'unhyang had no choice but to follow. Clutching her skirt tails tightly to her chest, she slowly steps forward, her flowerlike body moving with bejeweled steps. The rough path through the mountain is narrow and steep. She walks as if going to the king's grave in Handan City, like the beauty Xi Shi of the state of Yue, like the character for gold on a white sandy beach, like a broody hen in a sunny yard, like a swift on the main beam of Taemyŏngjŏn Palace, like a crane in a grove of flowers, like a butterfly in a violent gale, like a carp pushing through the water. She treads lightly and softly . . . "

This is a section from the classic book version of the "Tale of Ch'unhyang." Its rhetoric does not aim at expression but merely at humor and the use of precedent in order to invoke an air of learning. As a result, when read aloud it sounds good and, for readers who have no awareness of literature, its good use of "letters" is entertaining. Those women and peasants who were the readers of old-style fiction were fundamentally lacking in the literary awareness that would enable them to read fiction as literature. When they saw a storybook at someone's home, the question of whose work it was or what kind of book it was never arose. It was a storybook and thus merely something to be listened to with their ears. The appropriate question to ask was who would be reading, and even then there was no need to listen to the whole story from the beginning. Going to listen to the "Tale of Ch'unhyang," a story that everyone knew, did not mean going to hear the story but to hear the voice that would undulate and interject words to make the story sound better. Just as we slap our thighs and call out "Oh good!" when we listen to brisk folk tunes, in front of the storyteller we slap our thighs and exclaim out loud, "That's right!" "How could heaven be indifferent to this!" "Oh, pride comes before a fall!" If we get drowsy, we make no effort to listen until the end but fall asleep on the spot, snoring. Such a crowd was from the beginning composed not of readers but of listeners.

The fiction that we also call storybooks should be understood to have developed as the librettos of readers addressing a crowd of listeners. No matter how fine the content, stories could not be read if their sentences were not written with a certain rhythm, and from beginning to end they had to be full of humor and exaggeration in order to respond to the simple tastes of their listeners.

That is why, however "literary" the content of some of these stories may be, we cannot go so far as to consider those sentences and that mode of expression to be fiction or literature. And that is why people like Ch'unwŏn have gone so far as to rewrite the "Tale of Ch'unhyang," as they find themselves unable to rely on the many other versions.*

I do not have space here to discuss in detail the varieties of modern fiction: the conte, short story, novella, and novel, and then, within the novel, the serial novel, historical novel, and nonserialized novel. This is no more than a simple explanation of the concepts behind them. The "palm-of-the-hand story" is a translation of the word *conte* and is shorter than the short story. If we think of life as a complete circle made up of many angles and slices, then the novel depicts the entire circle, the short story depicts one slice

---

* Ch'unwŏn is the pen name of Yi Kwangsu (1892–1950), author of *Mujŏng* (Heartlessness), which is often considered the first modern novel written in Korean, and a prominent figure in the history of modern Korean literature and nationalism.

alone, and the conte touches upon one angle that is even smaller. This metaphor is not completely accurate, but, if we assume its validity, then the novella comes in between the novel and the short story. The serial novel refers to a novel that is written in episodes of a certain length that can be published in the newspaper each day, and, recently, the "nonserialised" novel has emerged to refer to a novel not written under those constraints. The historical novel refers to something that focuses on a historical figure, event, or background, but, as it is a piece of creative writing rather than an artistic lecture on history, it seems more often to be distinguished simply according to whether it is a novel or a short story. A problem seems to arise when, because the label historical fiction has been affixed, the writer himself feels bound to the historical chronicles, and readers in turn look for something more true than those chronicles or even try to force the writer to follow the chronicles.

No matter what the type of fiction, we must call attention to the fact that modern fiction is in general splitting into two paths. To put it from the point of view of the writer, there is fiction that we choose to write and fiction that we are made to write. The quantities may be small, but even in Korea newspapers and magazines are being published. As these are not purely artistic institutions, they have no reason to conceive of their editorial work as part of a literary movement. The continuity between one day and the next in daily newspaper news is weak. It is the serialized fiction, more than news articles, that has the strength of continuity to make someone who reads today's paper wait for tomorrow's. Newspaper and magazine editors do not look at fiction as literature, but as the crucial bait that will retain current readers and lure in new ones. Just imagine if either the *Tonga* or *Chosŏn ilbo* were to suddenly halt the serialization of all fiction. How many readers would stick with the paper that no longer serialized fiction? Our situation is not the same as in Japan, where last year the *Tokyo Asahi* serialized Nagai Kafu's *A Strange Tale from East of the River* and readers in Tokyo alone increased by twenty thousand. But in the case of Korean newspapers too the influence of fiction on circulation figures is certainly increasing. Newspapers and magazines will use fiction by any writer who has made something of a name for himself. Even if we know we are being used, we have no choice but to pick up our pens for the fiction we are made to write, as we cannot survive financially on the proceeds from the kind of fiction that we choose to write.

"Is there any law that says it cannot be a good novel just because it is published in the newspaper?"

There are certain important conditions of these novels: the serial novel must end at a certain length every day and its simple content must leave a strong impression that will remain in all kinds of readers' heads for twenty-four hours; it must create a sense of attraction that will make readers wait anxiously for the next installment; it must be of a kind that, if you happen to read even one installment in a paper that was used merely for wrapping, you will have to immediately subscribe to that paper because of that novel; and so each installment must be easy to follow; it must feel as if it has a new beginning and then, after some intrigue, it must end in a way that makes the reader think the next installment will bring some kind of resolution. Furthermore, the majority of readers of Korean newspapers are people who barely read *han'gŭl*, whether male or female. As a result, the aforementioned strong impression and attraction must take the measure of the interests and cultivation of this majority of readers. A novel that could satisfy all these conditions as well as the writer's creative desire is almost a fantasy. That is why it is appropriate to leave these serial novels to their own path and seek the possibilities for development of fiction as pure literature in the short story and nonserialized novel, which are not encumbered by these conditions of serialization.

The Taste of Fiction

There is no particular law as to how we should read fiction. But even when eating a fruit as simple as the watermelon, we use the phrase, "licking the surface." If we do not read well, there are times when we do not manage even to lick the surface of the work.

When pondering whose words to heed for a shortcut to a full understanding or appreciation of a particular work, our first answer would probably be those of the writer of that work or a first-rate critic. But neither of them seems to know as much as we the reader. On their own work, writers seem to be only more in the dark. If we read only according to the writer's instructions, then we remain unaware of the work's weaknesses and may not be able to discover strengths the writer himself had not realized; in short, we will not be able to rise above the literary knowledge of that writer. The critic, as a spokesman for the reader, is in the final determination no amalgamation of the people, but an individual limited by his own knowledge and sensibility who has his own specialist techniques with his own angle and mode of examination. Just as it is not necessary to be equipped with the knowledge of physiognomy or medicine in order to interact with people, the critic's specialist knowledge carries the danger of drowning us in insipidity when reading.

So, how should we read fiction? I have one simple point that I would like to make. Fiction, along with all other arts, is a form of "expression."

What will be the fate of the protagonist? How will this incident draw to a conclusion? These are secondary problems. If we read on, these questions will all be answered. But we have to know that there is a crucial aspect to the modern fiction we read for pleasure. A painting such as Millet's *The Angelus* is all content. Ordinary people can easily understand and enjoy this painting because it centers on the dramatic content of a young couple giving thanks for their pure and simple life with the sound of the dusk bell in the background. The content of a painting such as Van Gogh's *Sunflowers*, however, amounts to nothing more than a few sunflowers stuck in a vase. There is nothing in the least theatrical about it. As a result, ordinary people do not know how to enjoy it, and yet it is considered a famous work of art. How did Van Gogh see those sunflowers? How did he express what he saw? Van Gogh's own individual eyes and skill are present in the very lines and colors. It is the same with fiction. Fiction cannot be reduced merely to its content. As the level of cultivation of modern people uniformly rises, people are becoming too similar. If they want to reveal their existence in some way, they have no choice but to stress their individuality. Nothing is as necessary to the development of modern life as the encounter of individuals with individuals. There has been quite an increase in fiction writers as well, and so it would be pointless if they were all the same. An increasing number of writers strive consciously to emphasise their own colors, and their own special style leaves a taste that cannot possibly be found in stories from the past. This taste is usually dependent upon their eyes and hands. We can say, then, that in order to fully appreciate modern fiction, we need to know how to taste the talents of the writer in fictionalizing life. Of course, content has its own solemn existence. Ignoring it brings on fictional crisis. Paintings of mere lines and colors could possibly still retain their painterly meaning, but if we remove the content from fiction there is nothing left but letters. The ideal work is one where the form exactly fits its content. If content trumps form, the work is deformed, and likewise if form trumps content. We are misreading if we do nothing but taste the content and cannot read if we only taste the form. Yet, as the majority of readers do not know anything other than to focus on content, I would especially urge attention to the question of fiction's expression. To ignore expression is to fully miss the aspect of fiction on which the author exerted the most effort.

The Fiction Writer

Let us say that fiction records people's lives with dramatic content and a beautiful form. But the writer himself is human and thus material for fiction. He is himself buried in daily life, making it fundamentally difficult for him to transcend his situation and deal adeptly in his work with human concerns and everyday life. That is why some say one has to be at least forty in order to write fiction. If we take such a pessimistic view, only the gods would qualify to be writers, removed from everyday life as they are. Yet there are many fine writers in their twenties and thirties.

1. The qualities of a writer

I consider the essential quality of a writer to be sharp perception. Without perception he will not be able to discover those facts of human existence which lie below the surface stories that feed news reports, and, even if he does get hold of a complicated story, he will be unable to tie it all together truthfully.

2. Preparations for a writer

A writer has to know about everything under the sun. He has to observe carefully each day all the people who are the protagonists in the world and all the daily lives that are wrapped up in its length and breadth. Let us say that here is a kitchen maid. In order to see her first as a human being, we will have to describe her outer appearance, her way of speaking, her bodily movements, and other habits. Then we will have to observe such things as her work, her attitude toward her work, her desires in life, her saddest moments, her happiest moments, and the fate that awaits her. Only then will we be able to place her daily life in dramatic tension with reality. Of the person and their life, usually the life follows from the person, who is central. It is rare to find someone who does not qualify as a fictional protagonist once their views on life and the world are observed with interest and in detail.

3. Fictional expression

Once we have a grip on the personalities and events (daily life), then the problem of actual writing arises (the sentences). This is also a complicated issue. I want to stress this one key point: untidy commonplaces are of no use. There is no need for exaggerated phrases that are full of themselves. It must be description from beginning to end. Explanatory phrases that have no confidence in description are no more meaningful than annotations.

"The duty of the artist is to create, not to explain."

These words of Henri Matisse constitute an eternal rule for fictional expression.

Vague as this sounds, the art of excellent fiction is to find a person or a daily life that has some kind of significance and to reveal this in one's own way.

All kinds of expression are also possible in a nondescriptive storytelling form. However, only with a form of storytelling that has begun with description and then moved beyond it can one rise above simple explanation and produce a story that is seen rather than heard. Furthermore, even if it is a full-length novel, from the very first word of the very first line it should actually read like a novel and not some kind of scholarly introduction, and the conclusion should be natural, like fruit that ripens and then falls. Fiction will never approach an excellent level of expression if it strives artificially to convey seriousness and exposes the hand of the writer.

Friendship Between Men and Women

Given the choice between two people of equal familiarity, it is always more refreshing for a man to meet a woman rather than another man. No long explanation is required in order to understand this. What comes first to mind is that people of the same sex are just too similar: they dress and speak the same, walk in a similar manner, their expressions and behavior are all but prints of each other, and, as they grow older, they yearn secretly for the opposite sex. The reproduction of the same cannot but be monotonous.

For a man, nothing is as different and as complementary as a woman. Korean clothes may well be all the same color, but women's clothing is an utterly foreign realm. So completely foreign is it that we cannot pull it onto even one arm. We speak the same Korean language, but women's voices sound as if they are from a distant land. We understand the meaning, but such words could never emerge from our necktie-clad vocal cords. When we first meet a member of the opposite sex, is it not as strange as meeting a foreigner?

For a man, women are foreign territory. Not a desert inhabited by black people and lions, but a beautiful, luscious, and fragrant garden on an isolated island. They are a paradise for which we long intensely. How many Robinson Crusoes are there in town who, unable to withstand their longing for the isolated island, leap into the water and paddle clumsily toward it?

Disparate things enjoy being together. Even pebbles, when different, can rub each other's edges. Heat arises from the friction and a fire is ignited; this is not only a truth of physics. Such heat easily arises between the opposite sexes, and a fire is born. What was stone between two of the same sex soon turns to coal between a man and a woman. It is precisely this effect of coalification that makes the heat of a one-year relationship between man and woman more intense than that of a ten-year relationship between men. That which burns tends to be blind. However much we call something friendship, this only exists before the fire is lit, for once even a corner begins to burn then the friendship is over. I often witness cases where both parties make an effort to affirm their friendship, the one insisting that the other is just like a sister or brother, but in a second a fire is accidentally sparked and the friendship burns to ashes, as if they both have the insurance of getting married.

Friendship is a matter of loyalty more than affection. It can be stronger even than the natural laws between father and son. Of all human virtues, friendship can be the most beautiful and determined. No doubt for young men and women, whose relationships produce so many side effects, it far exceeds their strength to build such a magnificent thing.

Men and women are not the most appropriate partners for forming such friendship. They are by nature more suited to love than to friendship. If we try to build a temple with the wood provided for building a house, we will only encounter trouble.

In the end, there is no need to force friendship upon the opposite sexes. If it comes about naturally all the better, but it cannot be planned just because of some attraction. Meeting as friends when there is an attraction is like wearing a mask. Friendship should not be the larva of love. Although there are many cases where friendship leads to love, to say that friendship is the state prior to love would be a violation of friendship. Both friendship and love are forms of affection. As they emerge from the same fold of paper, they share the same blood type and embrace easily. In fact, friendship between people of the same sex, and between women especially, only lacks harmony in biological terms and is often emotionally very similar to the condition of couples. That is why those who are especially sensitive to affection receive such a huge emotional shock when a close friend falls in love or gets married. It is proof that their relationship had already crossed the boundary of friendship. As a result, there has even arisen the term *homosexuality*. Love is the eternal enemy of friendship.

It is not only friendships between women that marriage destroys. Although rarely the case with men, it is common when it comes to friendships between men and women. Between women, the unmarried one will be sad for a while, but, to the degree of the women's cultivation, their friendship can soon be resurrected. In fact, there is a good chance that the impure elements of their past friendship will now be purified into something eternal. However, it is extremely rare in the case of friendship between the opposite sexes either for the friendship to be revived after one side marries or for it to be purified.

This is why it is difficult for a pure friendship without any trace of love to develop between a man and a woman in the first place. In our society it is still much easier for people of the same sex to interact in all kinds of places. In order to deliberately turn one's head away from this convenience and suffer the inconvenience of socializing with the opposite sex there must be sufficient reward. This is the fundamental attraction that exists between the sexes, and it originates in beauty. The discovery of beauty in someone, whether physical or spiritual, is more likely to be the first stage of love than the first stage of friendship. The love relationship is far more colorful than a friendship, and in it attention and controversy reach a higher level. At this point those who are brave seem to choose the shorter distance toward love, whereas the timid are pushed toward the long-distance course of friendship.

At any rate, a relationship between two of the opposite sex, which is remarkable enough to be called friendship rather than a common acquaintance, has to be understood as a kind of deformed child of love. As a deformed child, there is always some sentimentality attached to a friendship between both sexes. There is some meaning not fully exhausted, as if one is gazing at a secret zone that lies one step ahead or covering over a final page instead of reading it. This is because the basic ingredients for building friendship are lacking. It is the environment that governs that secret zone in the distance and that final unread page, rather than the personalities involved. Try being alone for a while with someone of the opposite sex who is not a biological sibling. Even if your friendship is stronger than the bond between husband and wife, given the opportunity, something rash will happen to be sure.

In modern life, interaction between the sexes is becoming more and more common. In this age we can no longer look west just because a woman has appeared from the east. And yet there is no need to instigate a friendship with a member of the opposite sex, who consequently lacks the raw materials for building a friendship. One should meet and, according to the recent phrase, "interact cheerfully," without plotting any deep connection that would particularly earn the title of friendship. If a mutual attraction becomes hard to bear, then fall in love with dignity, according to the proper methods and without any pretense.

I would certainly not want to deny the possibility of friendship between a man and a woman. Even with the wrong ingredients, we cannot declare that there will be no true friendships at all, for such relationships, indeed, do get formed, whether through family ties, personal connections, or between those with a significant age gap. We should, precisely for these reasons, consciously avoid being alone with the opposite sex, who are biologically different and thus suited to us. When it comes to men and women, it is an eternal truth that ten times the amount of knowledge and ten times the character are always weaker than one opportunity. Friendships between the sexes, I believe, will always require more guarded observation than even those youths prone to ideological excitement.

This Thing Called the Popular

Classical Chinese did not only exist in the East, but in the West too. There it was called Latin. The priests and upper classes transcribed their records in Latin sentences with Latin vocabulary. Documents both sacred and official were written in Latin. In the West too, the common people needed storybooks in their daily lives in addition to sacred books and official documents. Only the storybooks were written in the everyday languages of the people (although these were all derived from Latin), and so Italians wrote them in Italian, and the French in French. In place of Latin, with its powerful tradition, Italian and French were used to write such things as storybooks, like a dialect or vernacular that anyone could scribble down. They thus came to be looked down upon as "romance languages," in other words, "storybook languages."

The dazzling modern literature of today's Europe has in fact developed from these storybooks written in the formerly despised vernacular languages.

The Korean language that we use to write literature today could be said to be a romance language of the East (although it is not a development from classical Chinese).

These storybooks that were once passed around the rooms of farmhands are the great ancestors of our fiction today.

Everywhere modern literature, and the novels that represent it, are written in the vernacular language. This is where the secular nature of the novel lies. As a form that describes the daily life of millions of people in the daily language used by those millions of people, the novel cannot exist without being somehow popular in nature. This popular nature is, then, the nature of being social. It means the irrepressible organic nature of the various angles of relations between individual and individual. Without this popular nature, humankind would not be able to organize or act in any kind of social way. Not only the novel, but all kinds of great art can only emerge when this great popular nature exists. One regrettable phenomenon of late is the appearance of several novels that ignore this fact and, lacking any kind of objectivity, seem to consider the new high art to be that which has left the popular behind. Sometimes, because of such people, I feel a danger of works that are popular in nature being criticized as of "low quality."

In fact, when it comes to works of art, the so-called popular nature that is truly unwelcome is not the popular of all things that are shared but rather the insincerity produced by the writer who does not control his subject matter with his spirit but merely jokes about it for pure entertainment. To call something popular just because it includes a love affair or nudity reveals a terrible lack of awareness. Even when worse things than nudity appear, if the writer's attitude is passionate, it should not be objectionable. But, no matter what kind of sages and heroes are depicted, if the writer's attitude is one of conversational jocularity, then that is the so-called popular, which is lacking in sincerity. Today the word *popular* is often used vaguely as a substitute for *insincere*.

More than anyone else, it is writers who have the obligation to rescue the popular from this distressing predicament into which it has fallen.

The Taste of *The Tale of Ch'unhyang*

In general, we can enjoy *The Tale of Ch'unhyang* in four forms: as a book, as a film, as a play and as a sung tale.* Everyone has their own favorite, but for me I still find the most excitement in listening to the story sung. In other words, the other forms of expression do not yet seem to evoke the taste of *Ch'unhyang* as deeply.

The Tale of Ch'unhyang was not written down by one individual in a set period of time, but was refined over the course of several hundred years by the eloquence, gestures, and ideals of many. The majority of those people were singers. As a result, *The Tale of Ch'unhyang* is neither a novel nor a play, but a libretto for singers of tales. Because it is a libretto, it is only natural that the taste of

---

* *The Tale of Ch'unhyang* is one of Korea's most popular stories, which has appeared in many different forms since at least the eighteenth century. It is set in Namwŏn, South Chŏlla Province, and tells the story of Ch'unhyang, a young daughter of a *kisaeng* who secretly marries the governor's son. When he is recalled to Seoul along with his father, Ch'unhyang is ordered by the new governor to act as his *kisaeng*. She refuses, suffering torture, until she is freed by her lover, who has returned to Chŏlla as a secret royal inspector.

the tale emerges best when hearing it sung. What feels awkward or exaggerated when read as a novel develops in a necessary and fitting way when sung. The love scene, which seems so vulgar on the stage, has, when sung, the air of a virtuous lady in the *Book of Songs*. And then Ch'unhyang in Chŏlla Province dialect, well, that just seems like the real thing!

Putting aside the question of the fictionalized *Tale of Ch'unhyang*, let us consider the problem of the tale as a play. The sung tale is something that developed over several hundred years. It would be vainglory for the film and the play to covet the position of the sung tale in a mere year or two. Both of these forms—the play as a play and the film as a film—will have in their own separate ways to create completely new versions of the tale. Naturally, even these new versions will be regarded as *The Tale of Ch'unhyang* and, as a result, the sung tale constitutes the well from which we have to draw in order to produce the taste of *The Tale of Ch'unhyang*. For the play or a talkie movie, of course, one has to bring together the right voices of Ch'unhyang, her mother, Hyangdan, and Pan-gja, even if it means going to Namwŏn. What will be demanded is not so much research as discovering the "reality" of *The Tale of Ch'unhyang*.

Kisaeng and Poetry

Recent introductions to Korea never fail to mention the *kisaeng*, alongside the Diamond Mountains and ginseng. The old shape of the Diamond Mountains has barely been worn down, apart from the appearance of many new paths, and the flavor and attraction of ginseng is the same as before, only in new wrapping and with labels attached. What has changed are the *kisaeng*.

It was some ten years or more ago. I had just returned from three years in Tokyo when I went to Myŏngwŏlgwan one evening.* Nostalgic as I was for a Korean atmosphere, it was the first time I had ever sat down with *kisaeng*. Two entered the room. I fell for them no sooner had they closed the sliding door and sat down lightly to greet us with a tip of their heads. Even their socks were cute, with their somewhat unsteady steps. But upon a closer look I could not help but become more and more bothered by the way in which they had both tied their skirts with the tie of a rubashka shirt. Moreover, one had parted her hair crookedly to the side and the other wore her hair in *mimikakushi* style over her ears. When I asked her why, she just laughed, and so a customer sat to one side replied in her stead that this was more fashionable and better than a Korean-style chignon. He added that it was the latest fashion to tie the skirt with a rubashka tie or even a necktie. I realized that this defamation of the unique *kisaeng* beauty was the fault not of their own reckless behavior alone but also of their customers and of the age they confronted. As our group became more lively, yet another *kisaeng* appeared. With this one I was capable of being truly enchanted, down to the last detail. Her name was Little Jewel, and she was from the Yŏngnam region. Her rather awkward attempts to speak the language of Seoul made her, if anything, seem at odds with the times, and then both her jacket and skirt were made from white ramie with just a single embroidered leaf dimly shining on a pocket. She wore her hair in a neat chignon, with only a jade hairpin and ear pick for decoration, and carried none of the rouge and powdered paper that the other two would pull out from time to time. The *kisaeng* with the rubashka ties could sing nothing but the Japanese song "Bird in a Birdcage," but Little Jewel played the *kayagum* and, as there was no one among the *kisaeng* or the guests who could sing,

---

* Myŏngwŏlgwan was the first restaurant in Seoul to feature court food and entertainment by *kisaeng*. It was built in 1904 in Kwanghwamun.

she sang along to her own accompaniment. She was by far the most polite and modest, and her face too was paler and rounder than the faces of the other *kisaeng*, who fussed and argued even in front of guests. If she had one flaw, it was her lack of learning. She sang a *sijo* but did not appear to fully understand the meaning of the words.*

Since then, I have observed *kisaeng* on several occasions, but I have yet to meet one of Little Jewel's nature. It appears that *kisaeng* has become another one of those words with various meanings and that the real thing is now a classic.

Kisaeng are, on the whole, women belonging to the realm of the emotions. How interesting that in the past they were true poets! Even though only a few poems by *kisaeng*, such as Hwang Chini, have been passed down, they easily surpass the numerous poetic attempts of literati, and we cannot help but be surprised at the depth of the poetic knowledge they accrued. Even the recent sensationists cannot compete with the sharp sensibility of *sijo* such as "Ah, what have I done?" or "This long, midwinter night," or even of the Chinese poems such as "New Moon," or lines such as those in "Taking Leave of So Seyang," which read, "The flowing water harmonizes icily with the *kŏmungo*, while plum blossom seeps its fragrance into the flute."

I would not exchange one *sijo* for a hundred poems in Chinese. Because of the inveterate disease of Chinese writing, the mouths that sang in our own refined language were all but forced shut. Nevertheless, even if we just consider Chini, there are more than the five Korean songs that we know now—the two mentioned above as well as "Deep blue stream in the green mountains," "When did I lose my faith?" and "The mountain is the mountain of old." In the *History of Kisaeng* there is a poem called "Dreams of my love"

---

* The *sijo* is a short, three-line poem written in *han'gŭl* and originally intended to be sung. It was developed during the Chosŏn period.

by Hwang Chini.* The real gold of the original lyrics has been lost, but a translation into classical Chinese by a certain An Chijŏng appears as follows:

> To meet my love I rely only on dreams;
> I visit when I am happy and happily I am visited.
> I hope that, in another distant night's dream,
> We may meet on that same road for a while.

The more I think about it, this poem must have been as beautiful as "This long, midwinter night" in both its meaning and sound.

At any rate, we should celebrate the wonder that what amounted to no more than an individual expression of emotion was then raised to the level of literature and still provokes fresh excitement in all who listen several hundred years later. Not only that, these poems have now become a central treasure of our own literary classics!

There is no doubt that the five poems by Chini mentioned above are the original lyrics, but there are several words and grammatical elements that were most likely changed by those people who were later the first to record these poems. The first word in "Ah, what have I done?" is a little unfamiliar but still easily understood by us today. But if we look at the *Songs of the Flying Dragons*, which was written not so long before Hwang Chini lived, then the language is really different.† The exact form in which Chini sang and wrote down these verses will always be a dream for us! Here I will share my joy at having encountered one old poem in its exact original form.

---

* Here Yi is referring to the *Haeŏhwasa*, compiled by Yi Nŭnghwa (1869–1943) in 1927. *Haeŏhwa* literally means a "flower that understands words" and was a set phrase denoting *kisaeng*.

† *Yongbi och'ŏnga*, or *Songs of the Flying Dragons*, was a 125-canto verse commissioned by King Sejong (r. 1418–1450) to eulogize his six paternal ancestors and especially his grandfather, Kim T'aejo, founder of the Chosŏn dynasty.

It is a piece treasured by the master Wuich'ang and originally recorded by a certain Kojuk Ch'oe Kyŏngch'ang in the early Chosŏn dynasty.* Ch'oe transcribed a song sent to him by a *kisaeng* named Hongnang, upon his return from a period in the northern provinces as a governor, with his own explanation and even a translation into Chinese:

In autumn of the first year of the reign of the Emperor Wanli [1573], when I went as governor to the northern provinces, Hongnang was already there at the barracks. The following spring, I returned to the capital and Hongnang came as far as Ssangsŏng before bidding me farewell. When she reached the Hamgwan pass it was dusk and growing dark; it was then that Hongnang wrote this verse and sent it to me.

This is the verse:

Mwoet pŏdŭl kalhaigŏtgŏ ponaenora
Nim ŭi son taijasinan ch'angpatkŭi simgŏ tugo posyosyŏ
Pambiye sae nipkot nagŏdan naringado nŏgisyosyŏ

I break off this branch of the mountain willow
And send it to you.
Plant it outside your window
And look upon it.

---

* Wuich'ang is the pen name of O Sech'ang (1864–1953), an accomplished calligrapher and one of the signees of the 1919 Declaration of Independence. In 1928 he wrote the *Sŏhwajing* (Evidentiary account of painting and calligraphy), a book that recorded, chronologically, the great artists and calligraphers of Korea. Ch'oe Kyŏngch'ang (1539–1583) was an accomplished poet and government official.

When new buds form after a night's rain,
Think that they are me. [*Hongnang*]

THE CHINESE TRANSLATION

I break off this willow and send it one thousand miles to my
    love.
For my sake, try planting it in the garden in front of your room
    and
Take note of the leaves newly sprouted of a night.
Haggard with grief, brows knit deep in thought, they are your
    maiden. [*Kojuk Ch'oe Kyŏngch'ang*]

After that, I heard nothing more. In the third year [1575] I was very
sick and unable to rise from my sickbed from spring through
winter. When Hongnang heard about this, she immediately set
off and finally reached Seoul after seven days and nights. At that
time it was forbidden for people to leave the northern provinces.
Although the period of state mourning was over, they were not
normal times and because of this her visit sparked many a ru-
mor. I lost my position and Hongnang was forced to go back to
her hometown. At our parting I wrote this down.

[*In the summer of the fourth year, Kojuk the sickman*]

Upon hearing that her lover was sick, Hongnang had departed
immediately and traveled seven days and nights. Even though he
lost his position on account of her, all he felt was gratitude for the
love that brought her to him. Still on his sickbed, he picked up his
brush, translated the verse that she had sent from Hamgwan Pass
when they bade each other farewell, and then wrote these details
down with a proper brush on writing paper to pass them down
through his family. It is a beautiful romance.

In Hongnang's verse *kalhaigŏtgŏ* seems to mean *karyŏ kkŏgŏ* [to choose and break off], *taijasinan* must be *taeisinŭn* [reach], and *naringado nŏgisyosyŏ* is *naingado yŏgisosŏ* [think that they are me]. The meaning is more profound than clear, and such sounds as *kalhaigŏtgŏ, taijasinan, naringado* are more gentle than our language today. If we had those beautiful verses by Hwang Chini word for word as they were originally sung, I believe they too would reveal this strange beauty of profound meaning and a smooth but crisp sound.

Kisaeng were comparatively free to recite these emotional things, but what enabled them to compose these songs in their own language was the art of singing, in other words, music. If there had been no songs such as *sijo* and *kasa*, then there would have been no reason to write poetry in our language, and even if they had been written they would not have been handed down.

It was *kisaeng* who sang these songs. There were so-called male singers, but only because there were female singers. Poetry in our language did emerge and has been handed down to us, if only as a fragile thread. This is in large part thanks to the *kisaeng*.

Orchid

There is a saying, "Live not in one place." It refers to a life of infinite harmony, where each place at which you arrive is your home and each person you meet is your brother.

Yet, as a mere student who is not enlightened, it is hard not to feel attachment for my own home, having divined its auspicious location and fallen in love with it.

It has already been seven or eight years since, after several years of planning, I built a small grass hut, arranged some books for study and hung some paintings and calligraphy, along with a sign I had obtained that reads "The Pavilion of the Appreciative Heart." And yet there has hardly been a day when I have been able to enjoy things with an appreciative heart free from all concerns.

As I am still young, maybe this is something I should aspire to in the future, but I barely manage to read even one page of the evening edition after dinner before my pillow beckons me. How starving for idleness this life seems to be!

It seems a remote blessing to be "unable to sleep because of idleness."

With paintings and porcelain one only has to dust them from time to time and they are satisfied. It is the orchid that cruelly makes you regret ignoring it for even one day. For three years or so I had looked after three orchids—a not particularly valuable but beautifully fragrant "thread" orchid, a Fujian orchid, and an "eighteen scholar" orchid. They all froze to death as the result of just one evening's neglect last winter. Since I lost those things that I had attended to night and day, watering them, finding sunlight for them and wiping their leaves, I have felt an unbearable loss, as if a member of the family has left. Still in the depth of winter I turned all the nurseries upside down and barely managed to get hold of one "spring flower" and one Fujian orchid.

And then a thread orchid that Karam had ordered for me arrived a few days ago.*

I love the way the thread moves in even the slightest of breezes.

Nothing feels better than to wipe the leaf of an orchid when tired of reading or unable to write. Apparently there is a saying in China that we should wipe an orchid leaf if we feel like fighting with our spouse. It means that through our association with the prince of the deep valley, we can all achieve the harmonious respect of pure silence.

That is how an orchid can calm our hearts. And that is why we also have the saying "Cultivate an orchid, cultivate your self."

---

* Karam is the pen-name of Yi Pyŏnggi (1891–1868), poet, coeditor with Yi T'aejun of the journal *Munjang*, and connoisseur of orchids.

Night Flight

The tendency seems to have decreased recently, but for a while writers were abuzz with words such as *behaviorism* and the *spirit of voluntarism.*

It was around that time that I read Saint-Exupéry's *Night Flight*, as it was so famous.

The translation was by Horiguchi Daigaku, and, although I know nothing about the original, I was astonished by the adjectives in the descriptive passages, which spun off an air of classical beauty of the likes of Shakespeare.* Perhaps I had been too hopeful in expecting some kind of new touch in the sentences themselves. Anyone could produce the rhetoric that made me feel the sense of speed here and there, as befits the subject matter of flying.

What leaves the strongest impression upon the reader must be the character of Riber, the owner of the flying company. What we feel in him is "youth" and eloquent testimony that, given cool, collected emotions and the will, anyone can become an action hero. Just as the people of Germany call out "Hurray for Hitler!" upon hearing Hitler's speeches, after reading *Night Flight* I called out once inside my heart, "Hurray for Riber!" Readers will also enjoy the way this novel allows ordinary people who have not flown to experience flight in their minds, particularly the adventure of flying at night and sacrifice in the air, which is more usually material for a newspaper extra article. There is pure beauty, unparalleled in other literature, in the scene of the mysterious high sky on that final night flight of the Fabian, when it rose up through the rain and wind to find only a sea of cloud below and the stars and moon above.

We cannot talk of works of behaviorism having read only *Night Flight*, but we can sense every moment of the action in this novel. I

---

*   Horiguchi Daigaku (1892–1981) was a prolific poet and translator of French literature into Japanese during the early twentieth century.

believe that we can understand to a certain degree what a behaviorist novel is supposed to be and talk about the concept.

Like all new trends of thought, behaviorism caused a momentary sensation, giving all writers pause for reflection and nothing more. It was sacrificed, having merely left this virtue of provoking reflection, and did not manage to become a new principle for fiction.

That the behaviorist novel leaves the impression of being too much of a chronicle is a regression for art; it is the weakness of such fiction that it relies too much on fact.

Yet as a short-lived trend it should not be looked down upon; there is no doubt that for any writer this new French cuisine is well worth a tasting.

books

The only case where I prefer the Chinese character to the *han'gŭl* is with the character for book (册). It somehow seems more beautiful and more bookish than *ch'aek* (책).

Is the book something that we read? That we look at? Or that we touch? In truth, it is all of these. To say that the book is something that we can only read is far too cruel and primitive an evaluation. We are already past the time when clothing and housing served purely for warmth. If we have already done this for the flesh, then what about the book, which is the clothing and housing of our emotions, our spirit, and our thoughts? May the book be more beautiful, for it is indeed the flower, the angel, and the emperor of all cultural products made by man!

The book is more than a material artifact. Just as there are young girls with pretty faces and young widows with lonely eyes, its attraction is of many different kinds. Those picked off the new publications shelf, still fresh with the scent of ink, are like young girls . . . how could they be so fresh and sweet?! And those that we dust off in an old bookstore and emit a smell like underarm sweat have the pregnant beauty of the widow.

In bookstores I belong to the express crowd. Most of all, I want to possess. At the tram stop I undo the wrapping and step up onto the car reading the first page; the further I have to go the greater the pleasure. Once home, I am a cold-hearted owner, throwing the new book down with others, only to rediscover it on a sleepless night.

From time to time a friend comes by to borrow a book. I feel a kind of jealousy. Because usually I have only read a page or two of the book myself. And because that beautiful, long story it had wanted to whisper to me will be told to another man first. Then, several days later, when I have completely forgotten about it, it returns to me exhausted and ragged. My friends do not withdraw with a mere word of thanks but go so far as to pass judgment on it. In such cases I often end up losing all interest in that book.

There are some books I lend that end up as eternal Noras.

Despite this, I sometimes borrow books from others. There are even several volumes that have long passed their promised return date. But there is a separate book ethic, which states that he who lends books is as much a thief as he who borrows. To have borrowed one thousand books in one's lifetime and to die having returned nine hundred and ninety nine of them would be a most excellent result. But, because of that one remaining book, you would still be a thief. Only to lend one's books to others and never borrow from someone else is even more difficult than to return those nine hundred and ninety nine books out of a thousand. That is why, with books, neither borrower nor lender can avoid the fate of the thief.

And yet books are to be borrowed. Art and the truth should not be placed under lock and key.

And yet books are more than material artifacts. As when extending an invitation to a precious daughter or a lady, it is most rude to hold out hands that are dirty or sweaty. A book is a beauty who does not know how to wash herself.

In the case of books alone I hold a feudal view of women. They should not be too healthy and heavy. I desire those that are light and slender with soft covers like that chestnut-flower patterned paper of old, so that I can hold them in one hand and lie down to read. But might I add that I also wish for a book that will submit to returning quietly and quickly to its former condition after something has been placed on it and that does not turn its pages up or get crumpled.

Brush and Ink

I am writing this now with a fountain pen. I will probably be indebted to the fountain pen until the day I die, but no matter how often I repeat the word *mannyŏnp'il* 萬年筆, I cannot come to like this name, which means, literally, a "brush of ten thousand years." No doubt it is a translation of the English term *fountain pen,* but I cannot imagine why, instead of quickly transcribing it literally as *ch'ŏnp'il* 泉筆 [fountain pen], the words *ten thousand years* leapt out from somewhere. The convenience of having only to remove the lid in order to write at any time and anywhere, without the trouble of preparing ink, China or otherwise, seems to lie more in swiftness and simplicity rather than longevity. And yet someone insisted on using the characters for *ten thousand years.* If it was because man craves long life and what seems to be the almost eternal age of seventy and therefore likes *man,* the character for "ten thousand," then would it not have made more sense to use *mansep'il,* with *se* 歲 meaning "year of age," or *mansup'il,* where *su* 壽 means "longevity"?

This fountain pen has stolen something from gentlemen of to-day. Most of all, the ink stick. It was the most elegant and devoted of all our friends in the study. What else is as fragrant as China ink on paper? What color is as genuine and brilliant? Because of this fountain pen, the ink that enables paper to live forever, that is its blood, has disappeared from both our lives and the lives of paper.

The phrase "the customs of the times" always refers to that which is convenient. That is why, having lost this precious ink, he who picks up the fountain pen cannot avoid being both contemporary and vulgar. But if, having secured an occasional quiet evening, he tries to appreciate the calligraphy of men of old, how can he withstand the nostalgia for ink that arises immediately before the traces of that ink's powerful flow? Just as we might say "mountains are not only to be found in high places," the love of brush and ink is not only available to those who actually go so far as to write, but is a joy to be savored habitually when looking at brush and ink.

I believe the brush is an instrument to be devoutly appreciated. When I was learning to read at the schoolhouse, nothing was as enjoyable as a visitor's arrival. The schoolmaster would tell us to go outside and play. Of those times, the best was when the brushmaker came and would stay for several days. Watching him place his soldering iron into the brazier and then pluck a weasel's tail in order to make a brush was far more fascinating than playing house. To shape the tip of the brush, he would stick the hairs into a base and then suck on the end with his lips before making downward curve after downward curve with his fingernails. The sight was sincerity itself. When the brushmaker left, disappearing somewhere over the mountains, even the brushes he had made would look forlorn. How I wish that I had preserved even one of the brushes made by those brushmakers with their properly tied horsehair headbands, their wristlets, and their baskets on their backs wafting scents of pine resin, glue, and flour.

There is no reason why anything valuable should come to me, but someone brought to me, here in this far away eastern state, what was in name at least an inkstone from Duanqi, Guandong, cracked but in a red sandalwood box. One should always grind ink with great care, as if dictated by fate.

To me, ink is merely one kind of scent. They say that long ago in China, the homeland of ink, those who were weak at the writing required for the civil service examination would be given a cup of ink to drink. Since I do not have the confidence to write even one character correctly, perhaps I should drink ten cups. I only have the shameless contentment of grinding the ink, of wetting the brush, and of smelling the ink.

The famous calligrapher Dongpo wrote, "Heaven-given innocence, this is my teacher."*

Even before I pick up my brush, I am already playing in dreams of heaven-given innocence. With just a long-tipped brush and some fragrant ink, the Pure Land can be found anywhere.

Copying

At the mention of Wandang I followed the duke Sŏnbu, who spends his time rummaging around scroll-mounting shops, to a certain house in order to take a look at Wandang's calligraphy.† It was an eight-part folding screen in semicursive style mounted onto a scroll, and as we unfolded it bit by bit a heavenly elegance

---

* Su Dongpo (1037–1101) was one of the greatest poets and calligraphers of the Song dynasty.

† Wandang is the pen name of Kim Chŏnghŭi (1786–1856), one of the Chosŏn dynasty's most distinctive and distinguished calligraphers. Also known as Ch'usa, Kim was the object of Yi's particular respect. Sŏnbu is the pen name of Kim Yongjun (1904–1967), one of the foremost art critics and essayists of the colonial period. Kim was also a painter and contributed the cover design to the journal *Munjang*.

filled the room, removing all doubt as to whether this was the real thing with the writer's seal affixed or not. Reluctant to leave just like that, Sŏnbu borrowed some thin rice paper and copied two of the screens in pencil. One screen read, in large script, "The ways of Heaven are pure and strange," followed by two lines in smaller script, which read, "the manifestations of the strange ways in reality are cleverly likened to the lotus flower." The other read, in large script, "A fragment of stone alone in the clouds," accompanied by "the heart of a sage is like a jewel in a deep pool." As it was Wandang's work, not one stroke was sloppy, and the short phrases evoked a thousand fathoms of implication. With meanings as endless as the great ocean held in just two or three characters, and a majestic sculptural beauty in the shape and body of each one, there is no doubt that Chinese characters are far too great to be evaluated in a purely utilitarian fashion. We did not even copy the phrase "At the never-ending stream below the mountain, we make an offering to those in the mountain, and with the gourd dippers we brought along we each take the moon with us." I wanted to recite such phrases as a prayer.

It was the duke Sŏnbu who made the copy, but it was I who first tried to write it in ink on paper. There was no way that I could form the strokes as in the original. I felt as if I were watching a film in fragments, and there was no way to bring it to life. Yet, seen from afar, the simple shape of the characters at least was excellent. I am rarely able to be at home during the day, but at night they seemed even more alike. To write out these two screens of twenty-four characters took me more than three hours on two separate evenings. I was imprisoned for two evenings in the strokes that Wandang had brandished so freely. For two evenings I had experienced the power of his writing, his purpose and its aftermath. I was able to memorize the strokes as I became familiar with the way the characters for *heaven* and for *lonely* flowed. It was as if I were touching the beast that was Wandang's stroke of the hand. I realized that if we want to discern a painting or calligraphic style, we need to understand the style of the original artist. In order to do so, copying, rather than looking, is by far the shortest path. Trying to copy those twenty-four characters over two evenings gave me double the insight into Wandang's writing than looking at one thousand characters would have.

Discernment is the foundation of all forms of criticism. When it comes to literature, too, those weak in discernment will not be able to grasp the real nature of a writer or a work. If a critic only reads, then he is likely to receive only a vague impression. If he tries to copy that work, then no aspect of the work will remain hidden from him.

It is most surprising that copying has such a virtuous nature.

One Part Words

The saying "Ten parts heart and one part words" refers to the emotional situation where our heart is overflowing with love, but we are unable to put all those feelings into words.

It strikes me that this situation is not limited to the passions between men and women, but is true of all forms of expression. There are all sorts of situations, and not only states of embarrassment, when we fail to clarify what we mean and are paralyzed by an inability to find the right words.

Atop my stationery chest I keep a ritual dish from the Chosŏn dynasty and from time to time I look at it. It is not all that ancient, but it bears the traces of the everyday lives of people of old in its cracks, which spread out like a spider's web. On top of its sharp-angled octagonal base, a rim blooms naturally like a thin and luxuriantly smooth lotus leaf. It has a faint hint of Koryŏ jade green; it is as pure as a fish that has grown in freshwater and as wide as if it could support the whole sky. It is serene.

Sometimes people ask me what is so wonderful about this dish. I try to explain, putting great effort into my rhetoric as I have done above. But the more I try the more my explanation seems lacking. I do not seem to be able to evoke even one tenth of what is truly great about this dish.

This reminds me of a similar story about Duke Huan of Qi and an old woodcutter.*

Once, when Duke Huan was sitting at the top of his hall, an old woodcutter who had been making a cart in the garden put down his saw and asked respectfully what book he was reading.

When Huan answered that it was a book of the ancient sages, the woodcutter responded that the book his lordship was reading must then constitute the dregs of our ancient elders. Huan was angered by this handyman's impudence and asked him to explain what he meant, for he surely had no right to go on living if he called the books of the sages dregs without giving any reason. The old woodcutter spoke calmly as follows.

"As I am a woodcutter, I will explain with the example of sawing wood for timber. If I pull the blade of the saw too slowly it will be crooked, and if I pull it in a hurry it will get stuck and not cut downward. There is a knack to pulling a saw neither too slowly nor too quickly. This is something that I know from experience and according to my own sense. It is not something that I can explain in words and help someone else to do just right. I think that our elders of old might have died still holding on to what they really wanted to pass down to us. If this is the case, it is no exaggeration to say that the book his lordship is now reading is something like the dregs remaining from people of old."

I am sure that Duke Huan must have nodded his head in agreement with this, but recently I have come to feel keenly that sen-

---

* Duke Huan (d. 643 BC) was a celebrated leader of the Qi state (eleventh century to 221 BC).

tences and stories are all too incapable as instruments for expressing a certain realm of mystery. I have come to appreciate the Sŏn priests' idea that the Way cannot be expressed in words.

Nature and Books

Why does nature exist? I do not know. It is an eternal mystery.

Why is nature so beautiful? I do not know. That is also an eternal wonder.

Why can nature not speak? I know not this either. But that is its eternal silence and its character.

We know nothing about nature. We will never be able to dig up its origin or its history. Faced with its sacred being, all we have is a pious intuition and hearts that are like blank pieces of paper. Beyond intuition, it is not possible to either see or hear the essence of nature, and so the greatest ability we humans have in its face must be our intuition.

Just try expressing your honest feelings about nature! Is there any poet who can see and feel and sing of a mountain as a mountain, or water as mere water, without any regard for the literature on the Diamond Mountains or for man's murky history on Mount Paektu? Those who begin by leafing through books when they want to visit some scenic site have so little confidence in their own skills of perception that they cannot possibly be artists. They are merely insignificant clerks of scholarship and archaeology and not artists of a resplendent life.

The Diamond Mountains have existed in all their majesty since the very beginning of time, long before they were given a name. The names and legends of the Fairy Peak and the Bright Mirror Platform are a recent invention. They bear no relation to the original Diamond Mountains; in fact, they are stories without foundation. What is the use of worrying about seeing the Diamond Mountains of the rumored "model" or of the illustrations that calculate the twelve thousand peaks or twelve waterfalls? Whether it be the Diamond Mountains or Mount Paektu or any other mountain, they have all existed eternally, since remote antiquity. When water still flows and flowers and autumn leaves bloom and scatter on their breasts, of what relevance are books and legends? I am not so sure about antiques and ancient sites, but, when it comes to nature—that body of life that does not know how to die—writings are of no value whatsoever.

Often when poets take nature as an object in their poems or travel essays they are too tied to other writings. Their tendency to treat nature as an antique leaves an unpleasant taste with their readers.

Throw the books to the scholars! For the artist, everywhere must always be a new continent, a new world.

The Love of a Work

Yesterday I took the train from Kyŏngsŏng Station to Sinch'ŏn. A group of young girls, holding book bags on their shoulders and under their arms, were chattering away like a flock of sparrows, while one of them buried her face in her lap and sobbed. The other children threw glances at their crying friend from time to time but otherwise made no attempt to comfort her and kept chattering on about what exam would be held or not and when and making bets among themselves. The back of the crying child's patched-up jacket was heaving. I wanted to ask why she was crying, but just then an older female student who sat behind the girls seemed unable to staunch her curiosity and asked my question. The chittering sparrows all stopped, and one replied,

"She lost her needlework."

"Was she supposed to hand it in at school?"

"No. The teacher praised her when she handed it in. That's why she's crying."

The older student gently patted the crying child's back to comfort her.

"Child, what's the use of crying? Will crying help you find it? It's silly to cry over something that can't be helped."

This comforting voice resounded so clearly, despite the noise of the engine, that I took another look at its owner. She was quite grown up, probably too old for middle school. She might have powdered her face; at any rate, with her white forehead and cool eyes she looked fresher than the glass windows on the train. I looked up at the ceiling of the train, which had just entered a tunnel, and thought about the words she had spoken to the crying child.

"Child, what's the use of crying? Will crying help you find it? It's silly to cry over something that can't be helped."

Such words stood to reason. Crying would not help her find anything, and it is certainly foolish to cry when crying will do no good. But people are always foolish when it comes to crying. It was even more interesting to consider that these words were spoken by a woman, and a young girl at that, who should by nature be most prone to tears. This is not to criticize that girl so full of hope, but once she has thrown aside her school uniform for the uniform of humanity, she will no longer be able to say that there is no time for tears—whether due to emotional or other worries—no time when "crying will do no good."

Even after I had gotten off at Sinch'ŏn, I kept thinking about this as I walked along: "what's the use of crying? It's silly to cry over something that can't be helped."

However, as these words and their speaker gradually grew distant in my mind, in their place arose the little girl who had lost her needlework. She must still be crying today and feel sad whenever she thinks of that little work of hers she lost. Judging from the back of her jacket, with its multiple patches, she would not have been able to get her hands on a piece of colored cloth easily. She had probably bothered her mother or gotten something from her friends and then sat in a corner and been scolded for not looking after her younger siblings, but with all her heart and skill she had cut out the pattern, broadstitched, and hemmed. When the teacher praised her work over that of her friends, the little girl's heart must have leapt with an excitement she rarely felt before. Now that school was over, she only had to take it home and give it to her parents, boasting of her good grade, but she lost it instead.

For the little girl, this was no small event, and neither would her sadness have been small.

I have lost several of my own works. I think it was the year after Tohyang passed away; Sŏhae had asked me to write something for a memorial issue of *Hyŏndae p'yŏngnon*.* I was moved, as I hardly received any requests back then, and so I stayed up, one hot summer night, writing. I corrected my piece and corrected it again, around ten times in all, and then sent it to the publishers. Sŏhae did receive it, but then somehow lost it and asked me to write once more. I could not find the same passion all over again. With no other choice, I did write something, but it was not as good as the first version, and I had to suppress my dislike as I sent it off.

Then there are things, which have appeared in the newspaper or a magazine, that I forgot to cut out and keep or that I had cut out but still somehow lost. Sometimes, if someone visits and says how much he enjoyed reading a piece of mine, after he has gone I look for it to read again. On at least three or four occasions I was not able to find the piece I looked for. And then it is almost impos-

---

* Na Tohyang (1902–1926) was an early pioneer of the short story form who died prematurely. Ch'oe Sŏhae (1901–1932) was also a writer of short stories and member of KAPF (the Korean association of proletarian artists).

sible to find the original newspaper or magazine once more and take a clipping. On those nights I have fallen asleep with no small amount of regret.

It was when I was writing my novel *The Madonna* that I struck quite a serious case of such regret. I had made quite an effort in writing about the struggles that the heroine Sunmo had gone through as a mother after giving birth to her child. I still feel a great sense of affection for that work, and, if it cannot be published as a book, I would like to be able to have it at my side, even in scrapbook form.

But I did not cry. I did not cry like that little girl on the train. Why did I not cry? Or, should I say, why could I not cry? It must have been because I did not feel enough attachment or devotion to that work.

It would be better to try to write a work of the kind that, were it to be lost, I would be unable to suppress my tears or stop myself from kicking and screaming.

Other People's Writing

From time to time I cannot help but wish my writing could be as easy to correct as other people's. In my own writing I fail to pick up on mistakes as obvious as incorrectly used verbs, but in other people's writing even a slight mistake with an adverb immediately leaps out before my eyes and is not easily passed over.

"Why do you look at the speck of sawdust in your brother's eye and pay no attention to the plank in your own eye?"

These words of Jesus are a good lesson for those dedicated to the way of writing.

Is it because we are blinded by affection for the writing to which we give birth, just like our children? When someone says, "there's something wrong here," even though we try to listen with gratitude, the truth is our first emotion is that of displeasure. Accepting criticism with gratitude is an etiquette that comes later, with the strength of cultivation. A heart that can look at my own writing as at that by others . . . I have always known that such a heart is necessary, but it has not come to me easily. Perhaps the study of writing can only be achieved with the spirit of seeking the Way.

Today, when once more there are forty essays placed before me, I am suddenly struck by my envy of art teachers. Even one hundred drawings would be easier to grade! But, with these essays, I must not pass over even one tiny little letter of those multitudes that spread themselves out knowing nothing of economy. Each one has to be read out loud. Each must be scrutinized and compared to the others. With both drawings and essays, there is the same obligation to look, but for drawings the grade is determined on the basis of examining appearance, whereas, with writing, could we not say that grading is like a physical examination? Writing is not something that you can just spread out, take a quick look, and declare to be this or that.

For these reasons, pictures are always easier than writing. With art, we can walk into an exhibition hall and, in two or three or four hours, we can perfectly appreciate several hundred works of art. But with literature, and something like *War and Peace,* for example, we have to wrestle with just one work for several days and nights.

Is it not strange that such writing, such literature, has preserved its dignity even in this age of speed?

There is no duty more unpleasant than having to assign grades to writing. It would be OK if we could just proceed with comments such as "this part is good" or "how about making this kind of change?" but, as teachers, we are forced to assign grades.

There is, however, no calculable grading standard for writing; it is not like science where so many points can be allotted each question, depending on whether the answer obeys the formula or not, and where a scientifically accurate grade can be assigned. Even though

I give 90 percent as a grade, I cannot make any logical pronounce-ment as to why. In general, as these things are managed by our emo-tions, writing will always be given inaccurate provisional grades.

Of course, the student who receives a low grade will be dis-pleased, nor does the teacher find pleasure in having to give a low grade, though it may seem cold-hearted, just because there are several layers of students at a higher level who did better work. Perhaps students do not realize that when we are returning work and call on a student whose paper we have given a low grade, our hands move reluctantly, as though we were offering a guest unap-petizing food.

Whether it be on the basis of talent or for behaving well or badly, it is never easy to judge others, nor does it seem a good endeavor. How they must suffer who say to others,

"You are sentenced to life imprisonment!"

"You are sentenced to death!"

After Illness

Illness

Sometimes when daily life grows monotonous I think, "If only I were a little sick." Occasionally I catch a cold, but it feels like a com-mon illness that anyone can catch, rather than a proper malady. It is messy too. Whenever I think it might be nice to take to my sickbed, it is malaria that I have in mind. While I was in Tokyo, now some eight or nine years ago, I suffered several bouts of malaria over the course of two or three years, and in my experience it was one of the most pleasant sicknesses, having something of the beauty of sport. I would suddenly begin to shake, and the shivering would be akin to when the count is full on the opponent and our pitcher has three balls and two strikes. Not even a father's arms could be so snug and comfortable and make every other desire disappear as did the feeling of lying down in the warmth beneath my quilt! Next there would come the sudden change, like a rain shower, and the fever! Then the silence in the dead of night after the fever had passed through like an express train! As effervescent, as chilly, as lonely as love, that is Miss Malaria! The speed at which she flies through the polar regions and tropical zones, and the utter silence she leaves in her wake, like an empty sports ground . . . this is what it means to be ill. It is like a love affair or a sport.

But that kind of malaria did not visit me again, instead I just came down with a bothersome cold from time to time, and then somewhere I caught this thing that extremely dull people pass back and forth like curses and I was laid up for fifty or sixty days. What an ignominy! Ha, ha!

Flowers

Some thirty days after I had taken to my sickbed, the most severe symptoms had passed. I still had a slight fever, which hovered around thirty-eight degrees, and emotionally I was tired, but I also felt at leisure. More than anything, I wanted to look at something different. I did not have the energy to read a book or the newspaper, and, though I gazed at the wall, it was always that same old wall. The pictures and calligraphy had become so familiar that I had grown sick of them. If I closed my eyes, I felt stifled, and if I opened them I still felt stifled. I longed for something new on which my eyes could linger and rest. If only there were something that could rinse them afresh like water. I placed my few old vessels in front of me, each in turn, but even grew tired of looking at them. Then one such morning, when I opened my eyes, my spirits suddenly revived. There, where my eyesight would most naturally fall, was a radiant flower garden! My eyes fumbled to count the stems and discovered no more than three or four carnations. White, red, and pink, they looked even sweeter to my eyes than food, for which I was famished. I asked my wife to bring the flower vase closer and then I asked who had sent them. Although my illness was one that people spurn, and the doctor would allow me to see no one, several dear friends had visited me bearing various gifts. When I asked which friend had brought these flowers, I learned that my wife had gone out herself to buy them. I was happy to have recovered enough for her to be able to go as far as the department store and also discovered a rare freshness in my wife, as in our younger days. Those bright carnations sat in the vase for several days smiling, like young girls from the West. The beauty of flowers is such that even when gazed upon for several days they do not repulse; the pure and fragrant oxygen that they emit, once inhaled through my nose, worked as a fine tonic for my cold body.

Faith

I was terribly afraid during this illness. When I thought of how Sim Hun, even with his model robust body, had died in an instant from the same illness, my thoughts did not remain at the level of thought but crept into my dreams, in the form of the scene of me standing vigil throughout the night by the side of his dead body and of the cremation, which had taken place no more than twenty days earlier.* Moreover, the book that I happened to be reading as I took to my sickbed was called *The Religious Man,* and, according to the afterword, its author was a young scholar who had also died before his time from this precise illness. Such inauspicious memories quietly oppressed me.

From the beginning, my doctor seemed to have sensed the situation and urged faith, even before medicine. He had earned

---

* Sim Hun (1901–1936) was a novelist, poet, and filmmaker whose most famous and popular novel, *Sangnoksu* (Evergreen tree), depicts the student movement to promote literacy in the countryside of colonial Korea.

a reputation as a scholar who denied the absolute power of the germ, voicing his opposition to the German doctor Koch, who had discovered the cholera germ. He said that he had drunk a whole cup of cultured bacteria with no adverse consequences, let alone death. He had done this, he said, not so much from any competitive desire to defeat Koch's theory but from his own firm faith in the human body's capacity to resist germs, no matter how many of them enter it; and so he had drunk some hundred million bacteria and, with just a few side effects, his body had recovered immediately, or so he said. You would not believe how much strength I gained from this story. I came to truly believe that, "no matter how thickly those germs swarm in my body, if my strong mental powers could only shine through they could kill more bacteria than the power even of the sun."

Then, one evening as midnight approached, the worst symptoms made their appearance. I did not myself find out until several days later, but all of my copious evacuations were bloody. I tried to speak to my doctor, but my tongue had stiffened. My hands seemed terribly cold, and, when I looked at them, they were as white as paper. Soon, I could no longer raise my hands, and, when I tried to move them, I discovered that my fingers had also lost all sensation. My wife and the doctor were whispering something out on the deck. After whispering for a while, they came back in; the doctor picked up his overcoat, and my wife her coat, and they both left. This time all I heard was the sound of the front gate. I sensed that they had gone to buy urgent medicine. They say that someone came to sit with me, but I knew nothing of it and thought that I was going to die alone. Once my thoughts turned to dying, I already began to lose consciousness. Thus I was unable to give a single thought to anything as practical as a will. All went dark. There would be a brief moment of brightness when I returned to consciousness, but then I would be dragged away again in battle. Yet, surprisingly, I could clearly hear the words of the doctor in the midst of that battle, which took place as though I were in a heavy fog.

"Keep your faith. Illness is not a crime but a test from God."

I certainly drew strength from this. "It is not yet time to die. I have done no wrong." This seems simplistic, but I remember that some strong mental power rose up from somewhere. With that strength I fought to hold onto consciousness, even though it seemed as faint as the moon's halo. One minute, two minutes . . . that tedious and most difficult period lasted only forty minutes, I later discovered, but it felt never ending, more like the span of one or two months.

That oh-so-faint consciousness was my spirit held in suspended animation. It was only after I received an injection from my doctor that I returned to full consciousness again.

If, in the midst of that dark, dark consciousness, I had not been able to sense those words of the doctor that I had previously drummed into my ears, then I might have remained in the dark forever. Perhaps that is what constitutes death. Needless to say, the doctor's theory of faith had turned into a resistance more powerful than any medicine, not just at the peak of crisis, but from before and after it too. Now that I am completely recovered, if I were asked whether his theory of faith was useless I would have to disagree.

There is a saying that a medical doctor cures sickness, whereas a holy doctor cures our mindset as well.

Truth

For the most part, the medicine that I took during this illness was the kind that has to be boiled. On the night that my body temperature had fallen completely, I received Western medicine—glucose and injections to stop the bleeding—but it was the power of Chinese medicine, boiled up three times during the night, that helped raise my body temperature all the way down to my feet. My doctor had made some slight changes to the main medicine that I took, according to the course of my illness, but the original prescription is said to be from some famous Song dynasty doctor. I was extremely impressed upon hearing this. Is it not miraculous that a prescription some person from a faraway land had written down in ink in ancient times had brought me back from the brink of death here and now?

The truth is that whose value never dies. And that is what constitutes goodness too.

Health

Having experienced this illness, I am now suspicious of perfect health. While I was recuperating, for some several weeks, I would sleep in the early evening for three or four hours at the most, and then I would pass those all too long winter nights wide awake. During those tedious hours I concocted plots for several novels. They were almost all tragic, and, several times, as I sounded out some conversations between the characters, I found myself crying as if I myself were one of the protagonists. There were several ideas that I was convinced I would write down as soon as I recovered.

Now that I can pick up my pen again, none of these novels seems to be worth writing: they all seem too cheap and sentimental. I thought it was because I had dreamed them up while sick, but I cannot laugh it off so simply, because there are so many pieces I have written in good health only to later wonder how on earth I could have considered them to have the makings of a novel. Now I am well again, but I cannot guarantee that I will never look at what I write today and hear myself say, "You call that writing!"

I wonder when perfect health will ever reach my mind? The thought is disheartening. Perhaps this is the lament of all ordinary people.

On the evening of the fifteenth day of the year of the Red Ox [1937]

The New Bride and an Ink Painting of Bamboo

One summer, a few years ago, I visited my hometown and came across two old books. They were written in Chinese and titled *Collected Writings of Taesan* and *Collected Writings of Kyŏmwa*. A quick glance at both front pages taught me that Taesan was the nom de plume of a man named Kangjin and that Kyŏmwa was Sim Ch'wije, but there was no way of knowing just who these people were. Moreover, as the collections were not dated according to the Western calendar but marked "the year of the red sheep" and "the year of the yellow dragon," I could not even tell when they were written. But I was most attracted to the beautiful characters printed in Song dynasty style in Taesan's collection, as well as to the sincere woodblock print of Kyŏmwa's collection, and browsed through the pages as I returned home on the train. *Collected Writings of Taesan* consisted mostly of poetry, whereas *Collected Writings of Kyŏmwa* contained poems, letters, admonitory precepts, forewords, commentaries, and various other writings, suggesting that Kyŏmwa was more of a Confucian scholar than a poet. Nevertheless, among the titles of his poems was one so lengthy that I read it before all the others.

Composed upon being moved by the young bride from Inch'ŏn, whose family was honest but poor and who brought in her dowry chest just one ink painting of bamboo by Kim Hasŏ.

The poem read as follows:

> A slave girl carries the single chest of clothes,
> And a pair of ink bamboo trunks beats a thousand pieces of
> gold.
> If our house is blessed with a giraffelike son,
> It will surely comfort this heart that has sought the Way all its
> life.

Such a father-in-law for such a daughter-in-law, one might say.

I only read it through once, but both the title and verse of this poem keep coming to mind.

Kim Hasŏ is an unknown painter whose name does not even appear in the *Evidentiary Account of Painting and Calligraphy*.* At that time his ink paintings were probably worth no more than a couple of pennies. But it was a virtuous time when the pure bamboo shade was constant and the father had given the painting to his daughter, who, as a good child holding virtue in esteem, had made an honorable marriage with just that one ink painting in her otherwise empty dowry chest. I yearn for such kindness, purity, and innocence. I can only regard that father-in-law with reverence, for knowing how to accept so sweetly the virtue and sweet etiquette of such a young bride and in-laws. I doubt that I could find such a high degree of virtue and culture in our modern families, modern culture or modern women. "A pair of ink bamboo trunks beats a thousand pieces of gold" and "It will surely comfort this heart that has sought the Way all its life" are lines worthy of our grinding down precious musk and highlighting.

We could refer to an endless number of unofficial histories, but the wife of Chŏng Sudong is the first woman who comes to mind in this regard.† Sudong was a strange man: he had no time to lament the situation when his wife worried about the rain leaking through the roof of their house; instead he watched the drops of rain falling here and there and began to sing the *Song of the Xiang and Xie*

---

* The *Evidentiary Account of Painting and Calligraphy* (Sŏhwajing) was written by O Sech'ang and published in 1928. It describes Korea's greatest painters and calligraphers in chronological order from the Silla period to early modern times.

† Chŏng Sudong (1808–1858) was a poet, friend of Kim Chŏnghŭi, known for his sharp satire and criticism of authority. He chose a poor but carefree life and eventually died from overdrinking.

Rivers: "An urgent situation at the end of the eaves, as one hundred waterfalls gush down . . . " After he passed away in someone else's home, a gentleman who had treasured him sent his widow rice and firewood when the winter grew harsh. But Sudong's wife refused to accept these offerings. The gentleman was astonished and asked his servant,

"Why did she say she would not accept it?"

"She asked who had sent it, and when I replied 'my master,' she said that your lordship had no obligation to send her fuel and food."

The gentleman slapped his thighs,

"Oh, what a mistake! Go back quickly and don't say that I sent you. Say that the mistress of the house sent you."

Only then did Sudong's wife accept the rice and wood.

The height of cultivation, manners, and self-respect lies in this ability to uphold consideration and etiquette, even when shivering and hungry.

There can have been no age before this modern one when words such as *cultivation* and *self-respect* were so frequently used. But does this degree of cultivation and self-respect govern we moderns and our modern women with such certainty?

Readers' Letters

I can only be thankful for the interest, or should I say kindness, of those who read my unworthy works and then go so far as to send me their impressions, even if they are critical. In the past I have been so moved by a letter that I have read it through two or three times and written a reply on the spot. That was how genuine and simple I was back then, or was it that I had more time? Sometimes I push to one side letters that even arrive with a stamp for my reply or that ask advice on wretched circumstances, casting aside all sense of shame, as if we were old acquaintances, and eventually I even lose the envelopes. Should we just say that is how cunning I have become?

"I will reply by writing good works."

There are two letters I have received recently that I would like to make public. I will just pass on the contents of one of them. The letter informed me in a roundabout way that the skylark that had appeared in Ch'oe Myŏngik's story "Patterns of the Heart," which I had praised extensively in *Munjang*, only appeared to be a skylark, but was actually a bird called a *paengnyŏnjo* that is good at mimicking other birds. It also informed me that some years ago in a travel piece on Manchuria that I published in the *Chosŏn ilbo* I had used the wrong character for "slowly," writing "tedious" instead. I am truly fortunate to have such readers.

The second letter I will simply transcribe here.

I found the following postcard as I was rifling through an old book.

"A long time has passed.

We have moved to Sungi-dong. My wife rinses the rice, and I make the fire. . . . We are like children playing house. Will you come up to Seoul for the state funeral? If so, be sure to drop in and share a meal with us. All you have to do is bring the drinks and side dishes. Ha ha ha.

It has been so long that I send my kind regards with just these few words. Ch'oe Haksong."

I can almost picture the happiness of Mr. Ch'oe as he sets up home for the first time. The letter was sent to my father, and I am happy to give it to you if you would like to use it in your book.

What amazing news for someone who was a close friend of Sŏhae before his death!* How vividly he seemed to come alive!

---

* Sŏhae is the pen name of the writer Ch'oe Haksŏng (1901–1932).

Readers, please do not scold me enviously when I tell you that I replied immediately to this letter.

The Year of the Ox

There is a kind lady in our neighborhood who tells our family fortune each year. According to her, my new year's fortune this past year was that of a fish going into the sea from a stream. When I asked whether that meant I might die in moving from freshwater to saltwater, she said it meant that I would move from an impasse to somewhere wide and abundant. We all laughed merrily. Not because we particularly wanted to believe her words, but because, after all, something good is better than something bad.

I have forgotten last year's fortune, but I know it was not good. Moreover, it was the year of the red rat, and because everyone else was nervous we too, having not experienced a red rat year before, felt ill at ease. Within a few months, the February 26 Incident transpired in Tokyo, Ethiopia had fallen, civil war had erupted in Spain, and here in Korea there was a succession of frost damage and floods, so it did indeed unfold just like an ill-fated year. What with dozens of private Presbyterian schools all losing their principals at the same time, such a year would only have to repeat itself several times and our shallow-rooted culture might even drown completely. Last year was unlucky the world over.

At the individual level, too, it seems to be rare to find someone who ended this year happy, and many laid the blame on it being the year of the red rat. In our house, as well, I do not know how many times we blamed events on that. Just as I was thinking of publishing my novel *The Madonna*, which had occupied all my time over the previous six months, it was secretly buried, and the future looked grim for the prospects of continuing to write *Hwang Chini*. But the climax to our unlucky year occurred when, for three months in October, November, and December, three of us came down with an infectious disease, though we were unable to hang the rope warning off evil spirits on the door for all three of us at once. I have no idea why this year is named after the rat, but what kind of fortune could we expect from that animal?

When all three of us were fortunate enough to rise from our beds and put on new clothes on the morning of the new year, the joy in our home was one of rebirth. Moreover, as the new year did not belong to a treacherous little animal like the rat, but to the benevolent and majestic ox, our hopes were all the more enticing. On top of that our new year's fortune read "lucky," and so you can imagine our feelings as we greeted the year of the ox.

The truth is that I have liked oxen ever since I was little. Many of my friends preferred horses, but I was scared of horses and would not go near them. I would go right up to oxen, however, even a bull. Their eyes always looked more innocent than those of whoever held their halter. Oxen not only carried the sacks of threshed rice but also the wicker baskets full of rice cake and taffy. Then there was the tale of the soybean mouse and the red bean mouse, which my grandmother used to tell me: the red bean mouse's mother dressed him in new clothes and took him to the party, but the soybean mouse's stepmother told him he had to fetch water with a jug full of holes and pound a whole mat full of rice in the mortar. A toad quickly helped carry the water and sparrows dehusked the rice, separating out the chaff from the grain. The soybean mouse still cried because he had no clothes to wear to the party, but then a black ox appeared from the sky and produced silk clothes and shoes and even a palanquin in which to ride to the party. I still recall how at this point in the story I would be clapping my hands with joy and gratitude to the ox, as if I myself were the soybean mouse. And when I myself was orphaned and everyone was wearing new clothes on a holiday, I would secretly look up to the sky and hope that such an ox might appear before me. That was one of the secrets of my lonely childhood.

A *yangban* on an ox, bob bob
A *yangban* on a horse, bob bob*

This was the song we used to sing as children when we saw someone riding an ox or a horse. I recall that I preferred singing this song when I saw someone on an ox rather than a horse. Horses were frightening enough in and of themselves, but the people who rode them were generally not kind: the masters before whom everyone in the village would cringe and bow rode horses, and sometimes police came to the village on horses, with their long swords hanging down. Consequently, the words *yangban on a horse, bob bob* did not emerge easily if I actually saw a *yangban* on a horse.

Such frightening people did not usually ride oxen. Instead of a saddle, ox riders would perch on top of the grasses they would feed to their ox and whistle or sing songs such as "Sweet Sixteen." They were good people who, when teased with the song "*yangban* on an ox, bob bob," would smile happily and pass on by.

Maybe Laozi too was a good and friendly person, as it seems that he often rode an ox. In pictures of him leaving the gate of the secular city, he is either standing or sitting by the side of an ox. Somehow an ox seems to suit the status of a Daoist more than a horse or a donkey. For people who transcend the realm of those who inspire fear it seems the horse is insufficient, and the ox more appropriate. The ox is bigger than the horse and can bear a greater load.

The ox is benevolent. I do not mean by this the utility of his strength, his flesh, and even his bones, but his appearance, which makes him the gentlest looking of all animals. His horns are not a

---

*   *Yangban* refers to traditional Korean society's hereditary, educated elite classes.

weapon. He is big but not treacherous. In the tale of the soybean mouse and the red bean mouse the ox plays the benevolent role. When Zhuangzi said, "If you call me an ox, I am an ox, if you call me a horse, I am a horse," he meant that blame cannot be laid on the world's rights and wrongs, on good and bad, but he used the ox as a metaphor for the right and the good.

It is not just that the ox looks benevolent. He is always calm. His freedom from distraction is reminiscent of Daoists and virtuous elders who believe in "nurturing purpose by calming the mind." The ox must look like this to people in both the East and West, past and present, for there are many tales of oxen in *Aesop's Fables*, one of which reads like this:

Once, a mosquito was flying about and landed on an ox's horns to rest. After a while, the mosquito got up and spoke to the ox,

"You don't mind me resting on your horns a little longer do you? If so, I will fly elsewhere."

The ox replied:

"Please do as you wish. I didn't even notice when you came and sat on me. You say that you will go, but how would I even notice?"

This is the year of such an ox.

Trees

Our garden is only a few *p'yŏng* in area, but how grateful I am just to be able to stand amidst the trees!* Apart from some dozen cherry trees that form a kind of hedge, there is a persimmon tree, apricot tree, date tree, and peony as well as one or two white birches—these are all precious guests for whom my family must care.

---

* One *p'yŏng* is approximately 3.3 meters square.

They provide us with flowers, fruit, green shade, and fragrant air, and in return they receive nothing from us. When there is a drought, we give them some water, and when it is cold we wrap straw around a couple of trunks, but this is nothing, truly nothing, compared to the beauty, flavors, and fragrant shade they offer us. What friend or rich man would be satisfied with giving this much and receiving nothing in return? By way of these trees, nature nurtures us and teaches us many lessons.

The trees are standing in silence just now. It is as if spring is still several thousands of miles away. But if I stand beneath a tree I can immediately sense its approach. When I take hold of a branch, each of its fattening buds seems to whisper that it will flower with just a light evening rain and a morning of warm sunshine.

Spring, come forth!

Whenever I walk under the trees in winter, I cannot wait for spring to arrive.

Every time my family picks a date or a persimmon, or the cherries ripen, we think of the former owner, not so much for passing on the house to us but for passing on the garden. The persimmon tree bore its first fruit only after we had moved here, meaning that the former owner planted the tree and left without ever reaping its fruit. We do feel awkward, as if we are harvesting someone else's field. Several times I have recalled a short story written by a certain French writer under the title of "The Indian Cottage."* It tells the story of a scholar who travels the world in search of the truth: when he is finally on his way home, having failed in his quest, he encounters a storm and ends up entering an Indian man's hut. The hut's owner is a member of India's lowest class of untouchables known

---

* This is a story by Jacques-Henri Bernardin de Saint-Pierre titled, "La Chaumière indienne" (1790).

as Pariah and lives a life completely isolated from culture. But this Pariah provides the scholar with a clue to the truth that even the greatest monks and literati had not been able to teach him. I still recall this from what the Pariah said in their conversation:

> Whenever I pick a fruit and eat it, I always bury the seed in the earth before leaving that place.
>
> This is not so that I can come and gather fruit there again when that seed has grown. It does not matter who gathers fruit there. By doing this I am simply following the way of heaven . . .

How simple, yet how great this is! I have no idea whether the former owner of our garden also thought that he was following the will of heaven when he planted these fruit seeds, but as they produced several fruit trees, which both look and taste good and give us great joy in the harvesting, this is a blessing that my family can never forget.

Yet from time to time I change my mind and even feel somewhat dissatisfied. Perhaps I ask too much, but I feel it rather unfortunate that the former owner planted several small trees. Even if it means no fruit, I would rather walk beneath one large tree than several small ones.

The taller a tree the better. The older the better too. I can certainly appreciate the elegance of a small branch heavily laden with blossoms or fruit, but what I yearn for is less a tree I can prune than a tree whose canopy will cover me, my house, and even my garden and that will stretch up to the sky like a mountain peak, so that I can walk humbly beneath it and always be made to see just how small I am as I gaze up at it with big round eyes like those of a small child.

In the villages and gardens where wise and virtuous men used to walk, we usually see large trees. In the village in Onyang, where the duke Yi Ch'ungmu once lived, there is a hill where he is said to have practiced archery.* It was there that I saw two strapping gingko trees rising up to the sky like cliffs, although now half dead. I was happier to see that pair of trees than the knife, arrows, and other things left behind by the duke himself, and I bowed my head before them.

Although they were old, they were still alive. No matter that they cannot speak, those two gingko trees are the only living things left that were there alongside the duke Ch'ungmu.

The trees had grown freely over the course of many years. It looked as if it would require quite some arm strength to throw a stone up into their upper branches, especially as they stood on a hill. It was their height and imposing shape that attracted me. A dull common tree or a pine tree decorating a stone mountain could never be as precious as these two giants, even if the smaller trees had been planted by the great Duke Ch'ungmu himself. My head bowed down before these huge trees as they soared into the air like the faces of great warriors or mountain peaks.

Even if it means having only one tree, I would prefer to live beneath a tall one. Rather than linger between low fruit trees while licking one's lips, how much more noble it is to stroll with a pure heart and joy beneath an old tree shining brightly in the moon and feel only the refreshing breeze! To live in a shade as deep and green as the ocean in the summer and to let those leaves bury the entire garden and house in the autumn. . . . What a luxurious harvest that would be! How the wind would resound on a winter evening, like the ululations of the largest organ! Our lives may feel as if they

---

* The Duke Yi Ch'ungmu is also known by the name of Yi Sunsin (1545–1598), an admiral famous for leading the assault on the Japanese forces during the invasions of Hideyoshi at the end of the sixteenth century.

hang on a thread, but I would like to ponder my remaining days while resting beneath such a large tree and gazing up at the stars in the sky far above.

The last third of the first month of the year of the Red Ox [1937]

Plum Blossom

When my wife says we still must beat our starched clothes though it makes them feel more chilly, when the cold air penetrates even the closed shutters, and on those days when it is so cold outside that the soybean soup brings a welcome fragrance to the dinner table and the frozen narcissi lift their heads in the steam from the scorched-rice tea, that is when I feel the onset of winter. When my wife's red hands pluck chunks of ice out of the jar of cold radish soup, I can feel how cold it is without eating even one mouthful. It is because our body temperature is warm that winter feels so cold. If we were like the frosty snow or the plum blossom and the winter were warm, what would we do?

The snow on the mountain out front has been white for several days now. There are times when it feels claustrophobic to have a mountain so close to our deck, but lately it looks as if a folding screen has been wrapped around our garden. The dusky pine groves and the copses of strapping bare trunks are dense in places and sparse in others, creating a balance reminiscent of a work done in brush and China ink. A wander through this valley when the mountain shadows are at their longest, even if not on a donkey, provides some of the flavor that the Tang poet Meng Haoran must have experienced when going in search of the plum blossom.

Although winter should be cold, it felt too extreme when the temperature dropped so much that we could not even plant a plum tree in the garden.

In the deep snow of the next village
A blossom opened last night

When we read poems such as this one, it seems that the very nature of the plum is to blossom in the snow, but a Seoul winter freezes even the frost and the snow, and, after all, the plum is only a flower! My fondness for the plum stems first of all from my yearning for the refinement of gentlemen of old. Last autumn, I came into possession of the following piece of calligraphy by Wandang, although I have no idea who the original poet is:

A seeker of the Way, who is inclined to wander with no taste
    for sitting still,
Closes the door for ten days in order to wait for the plum to
    bloom.

It was my ardent wish that winter should come quickly so that I might place a potted plum beneath these words and shut myself away for ten days.

The plum blossom is not so much pretty as pure, and color is not its finest point, as it tends to be harsher even than that of berry blossom. Convinced that compound leaves drape heavily on the plum, I went in search of a single-leaf white plum, not yet in bloom, and that was where my problem began. I selected a plant with just a few buds that were still green and brought it home. But the buds gradually reddened as they opened into blossom and, to make matters worse, it turned out to be a compound leaf: possessing all the splendor of a peacock, how could my plum be a companion to this fastidious crane! I could not help but feel a little disappointed, until one morning I was greatly surprised. My wife had absentmindedly left all the plants in our round attic one night when the temperature dropped down to minus ten: the narcissi and orchids were badly frozen; only the plum, despite being red, cheered its owner with some lively pistils and stamen as distinct as a young lady's eyelashes!

Some call the chrysanthemum "icy frost," but its forbearance cannot match that of the plum. If our house had been properly heated, I would not have been able to understand the unwavering integrity of the plum, even if I kept some thousand potted plants. They say that the cold and poverty give birth to an integrity that emerges from enduring difficulties. If what they call love, life, and happiness are real, then I do not believe they will be found outside this realm of forbearance.

This coming winter I will try once more to find the single-leaf white plum that I failed to find this past winter.

The Classics

It is a fine thing to read through the new translations published by Paeksu Publishing Company, but sometimes it is also good to rifle through the moldy leaves put out by Sinmun'gwan or Hannam sŏwŏn. I sometimes hear of people who only read Western books, but then, amidst all the cries of "our classics, our classics," try to read our Korean books for one evening only to express their disappointment that very night. It is hard to believe one could sample even one tenth of a classic's nature with such a rushed reading, even if it were a classic from the West.

Koryŏ celadon and Yi dynasty white porcelain are not valuable simply because potters are no longer able to reproduce their green and white color. In fact, people who are not craftsmen are even more extreme in their prizing of the green of Koryŏ celadon and the white of Yi porcelain. This must mean that a classic possesses some interpretation or some sensation that transcends its production.

O moon, rise high
And shine far abroad

If we ask someone, singing this verse and slapping his thighs to
the rhythm, "Well, what is so good about this?" his reply will most
likely be no more remarkable than "It's just good, isn't it?"

"O moon, please float up higher and higher in the sky and shine
your light brightly into every deep valley. Make the night road bright
for my husband who is on his way home so that he may not lose his
footing and arrive as early as possible . . . "

When we try to interpret the verse in this way and even add ex-
clamations of admiration, such as "It's really quite a clever verse,"
we may be guilty of committing that arrogance of the moderns in
disdaining people of old.

O moon, rise high
And shine far abroad

Of course, this is a marvelous phrase, but we could equally find
such special phrases among the works of our contemporary poets.
Is it not belittling to our ancestors to be amazed that they could
think up such a verse?

The way of the classical spirit may rest forever in the idea of "re-
taining the old and learning the new," but this does not mean the
physical beauty of the classics is something that can be felt through
intellectual appetite alone. That is why the beauty of all classics par-
takes of the solemn nature of the antique. If we separate the beauty
of age from Koryŏ celadon or the Chŏngŭp ballad,* then what is so
beautiful about them?

---

* A song from the kingdom of Paekche (18 BC–AD 660) and the oldest extant
verse written in *han'gŭl*. The kingdom of Paekche ruled over the southwest-
ern part of the Korean peninsula.

"O moon, rise high"

Paekche resonates from within this one phrase that transmits the emotions of generations of real living people. With this nesting of the distant past, our lips can sing the verse and savor it.

Just as it is courteous to be humble before our elders, we should straighten our collars as we approach a pot or song because they are also old. Unless we approach them with the heart of one visiting a mountain temple, wearing straw sandals and carrying a bamboo stick, and not as if driving a car to a hotel, the classics will always remain a cold skeleton, and their warm hearts will not jump out at us.

If we try to interpret before fully feeling, we will not avoid being trespassers of the classics. Their classical nature is not something we can know, but something we must first feel. This is what I think.

A Poor Drinker

"Please don't drink," would be the earnest request of those who care about me.

"Please learn how to drink," would be the polite request of friends who know me well.

"You should neither force yourself to drink nor not to drink," is the advice given by some of my most trustworthy friends.

I have not really been torn between these different opinions and only regret that I was not endowed with a strong liver. I have no problem with "passing by the barley field without stopping for a drink," as it were, but if I do drink I turn bright pink at the first drop. Spoiling my friends' drinking is less my concern than how to avoid the derisive smiles my color provokes at drinking parties.

Most of my friends who write also like to drink. Ch'unsan, Usan, Wŏlp'a, Chiyong, Int'aek, and Hwaam, in particular, all have strong livers and meet up day and night.* There have been more than a couple of evenings when I have felt like a lonely shadow hovering on the sidelines.

I am not the sort to insist on disparaging the virtue of wine just because I am unable to follow the path of Liu Ling,† for how can we deny that alcohol is more than a mere drink when we pour wine for the spirits, as we burn incense to freshen a room? What I do despise is the so-called drink demon who harasses people to buy him a drink.

Those friends who press precious bouquets of wine on others as if it were drinking water do not know the virtue of frugality; those who drink with their muscles rather than using their minds and then want to engage in public displays of weight lifting are gatecrashers who invade the peace in the land of drinking; and those who become garrulous and entice those near them into keeping them company are not gentlemen drinkers. Nevertheless, sitting cross-legged in silence could hardly be called proper drinking manners either.

"How do you hope to live as a writer if you can't drink?"

Occasionally I am perplexed by this question, and it is true that if Li Bai, the Gentleman of Jin, or Omar Khayyam had not drunk wine, their poetic spirits might never have come to fruition. The literary eyes of old—in the world of both prose and verse—were telescopes that gazed upon the cosmos.

Perhaps it is fortunate for such poor students of drinking as myself that our modern literature has grown so shortsighted.

---

*   Usan is the pen name of painter and art critic Kim Yongjun; Wŏlp'a is the poet Kim Sangyong (1902–1951); Chiyong refers to the poet Chŏng Chiyong; Int'aek to the fiction writer Chŏng Int'aek (1909–1953). It is not clear who Ch'unsan and Hwaam are.

†   Liu Ling (221–300) was a Chinese Daoist poet, known as one of the Seven Sages of the Bamboo Grove. A notorious drunk, his most famous poem was titled, "In Praise of the Virtue of Wine."

My drinking capacity may be weak, but perhaps I am not totally blind to the laws of alcohol, for whenever a good friend visits my home I feel the urge to offer him a cup of wine in the place of my less tasty friendship and when sad I think of wine as medicine for an ailing soul.

There are those who slip gracefully into the land of inebriety, as if in a painting: as they drink, their cheeks take on a lustrous tinge; a peaceful haze cloaks their minds; they keep an eye on how much their friends are drinking and enjoy the wise talk of those friends. We might think of these drinkers as the saints of wine. They do not speak of its virtues, but are themselves those virtues. Neither is friendship something of which they talk, rather they embody it in all sincerity. Have the laws of drinking degenerated to the degree that we ignore such examples, only to learn disorderly conduct in their stead?

The suffering of the poor drinker lies in the drunken mistakes of his drinking companions.

The Carpenters

Now that materials are at their most expensive, we have finally begun to build our house that has been so long in the planning. All through the dog days of summer we have watched the trimming of timber and flattening of the earth, so that now I can actually feel in my bones just how precious a house is.

Of our five carpenters, four are in their sixties. One of them, known respectfully as Sŏndanim, always wears a horsehair skull-cap and could not be far from seventy. Apparently there is no carpenter in Seoul who does not address Sin Sŏndanim as Teacher. A famous carpenter, who once stood tall whenever a royal palace or a shrine was built, he makes his living by drawing the ink lines at each worksite. This Sŏndanim is the one who chooses the wood and cuts it. Our house is a smallish job of around ten *kan*, nevertheless it is quite marvelous to see how he measures everything so accurately on his hands, without writing anything down.

At first, I wanted to hire the carpenters on contract. Although my budget was barely sufficient, I did not have time to supervise them. But the carpenters said that they quickly lose interest in their work when it is on contract. What with having to worry about taking a loss and leaving enough for their wages, they lose all interest in the actual carpentry, and once that happens the whole job goes badly. I was moved by their honesty and realized that building a Korean house would mean savoring the simple and generous spirit of Yi dynasty architecture. As it would be impossible to express that tradition without the hands of these old-style craftsmen, whose affection lay in their work more than in money, I considered this a rather fortunate turn of events and decided to pay them on a day-to-day basis.

They are in many ways craftsmen who lag well behind their times. They wear horsehair skullcaps; they loosen their belts, from which dangle spectacle cases and tobacco pouches, all the way down to their groins; they carry bamboo fans and fairly long pipes—for laborers, that is; and they wear canvas shoes over their cotton socks. The two old men in charge of sawing wear straw sandals. There is no sign of those "towels" that have become so common, rather they wipe away their sweat with a black cotton rag. As for their tools, their saws, plane, adze, and ink pad case are all handmade and have no trademark affixed. Their conversations, too, are rich; here I will record a couple of them.

"Last year you know, I was doing a job over at Chin'gogae. I kept wondering what this *kochi kochi* word meant, but I've just found out that it's a nail."

"*Kochi*, a nail? Ha! You sure learned that well!"

"What is it then, this *kochi* thing?"

"*Kochi* is 'over there,' as in 'over there' . . . a nail, now that's *kugi*."

"*Kugi* . . . like, Hurray for the *Kugi*?"*

"Dear Gods, help me . . . "

They had barely even laughed before the conversation turned to another topic.

One day the old men were sawing and had stopped to wipe their faces and drink some water.

"I drank some expensive water once!"

"Where?"

"It was on my way home from a job over at the front of Kaemyŏng. Must have been the worst of the heat then too. I finished up work and was going home, but, lord, my throat was dry. That was when I found this thing . . . oh, what do they call it? It's all in these Western-type cups. They put a little in a cup, and all this crumbly ice and water. My, it was cool on the throat . . . "

"Ah, that must have been what they call *ashikuri*."

"Now was it some kind of *kuri*? But let me tell you, it was daylight robbery!"

"Oh, yeah?"

"Well, it was so refreshing I had two cups, didn't I?"

"How much did that set you back?"

"Well, it's just frozen water with a bit of sugar mixed in, right?"

"Frozen water. That's right. Not even hard enough to be ice. It's like they try to freeze it, but it doesn't freeze properly."

"Right, and in between these tiny bits of ice, as tiny as birds' eyes, there's a bit of water? And for that, they want twenty *chŏn*!"

"Twenty *chŏn*! No way."

---

* Whereas *kugi* is Japanese for "nail," *kukki* is Korean for "national flag."

"It blew my mind. How much water would you get for twenty *chŏn*? Maybe ten loads? And they're asking what we pay for twenty pails of water . . . the thieving devils!"

"That *ashikuri* thing sure is expensive."

"You bet. The whole summer none of us at home could drink water without thinking about it . . . "

"Whatever next!"

And then, once I overheard this . . .

"These people called doctors, I tell you, they're no different from shamans and blind fortunetellers!"

"How come?"

"They say they can tell what's wrong with a man, but how can they be such liars?"

"Isn't that all the mystery of nature?"

"Mystery in a magic glass, more like. What makes them think they can see what's inside someone else when the person who's sick doesn't even know?"

"That's right! The shamans may be useless, but we're sure to hold a good ceremony for the spirits come October."

"And why's that?"

"If there're no ceremonies, then how would the likes of us ever taste a rice cake?"

These old men said that they live somewhere over in Wangsim-ni, but they would arrive in this corner of Sŏngbuk-dong before sunrise and would not quit work until it had grown so dark that they could no longer see their ink lines. They are not as quick and agile as younger men, to be sure, but they are diligent. And they are as sincere as if it were their own home they are building. Their tools are not too sharp, but they get the job done. The traces left by such tools are blunt, but trustworthy and natural-looking. I am quietly and joyfully hopeful that our house, which they are building with their own hands, will not be shoddily built, however new it may look.

Fishing

With the recent development of sports, even fishing has been included in the category and is now spoken of in the same breath as baseball or golf.

This may well be the result of the naturally lively tendency of sports to socialize, but the profundity of fishing actually lies more in its spiritual than its physical nature.

A green mountain rises up in the foreground, with a stream flowing at its foot. This hilly spot possesses a certain calm, and one's footsteps loiter on the rocks.

When a quiet gentleman takes up a spot here for the day, it is not merely because he has an eye on the fish swimming by.

It is in order to be alongside the calm of the water, and to share in its leisure, its languidness, and its purity.

And it is in order to be with the fish. The joy of fishing lies not so much in catching fish as in being with them.

Although fish do get caught, fishing is nothing like hunting with a gun. The hunter chases the beast and shoots it, even as he listens to its screams, and finally he sees it shed blood. There is nothing so bloodthirsty about fishing.

It is true that fish get killed, but fishing does not involve chasing down a running beast with the muzzle of a rifle and aiming at its vital parts. The fisher must lure the fish toward himself through clear or cloudy water. If he loses the fish, then he simply smacks his lips in regret, and that is all. Unlike deer or tigers, fish do not scream. Once they make their way into the straw baskets or nets and start splashing about, it is a beautiful sight. There is nothing gruesome about it at all. Death comes as silently as sleep, as if the fish linger in a region where life and death are one like the sages.

From this perspective fishing is of a kind with neither sport nor hunting.

Fishing varies according to each region and the water, as do the words used to describe it as well. I have never lived by a large river. My own experience has been fishing in small valley streams, unnamed and unmarked on maps, that rise and fall with just a single day's rainfall. Thus all I know about fishing and its terminology is inevitably based upon our local streams in Ch'ŏlwŏn.

There are three kinds of fishing with which I am familiar.

Splashing

When the rainy season sets in and the water turns red, the catfish, eels, and mandarin fish, which usually hide beneath the stones, move in search of food into larger pools as they fill up to the brim. These fish tend to emerge more frequently at night than during the day, and so it is at night that we go fishing with the appropriate gear to catch these fish. The rods are about half a man's height and quite sturdy, even a thin ash tree will serve the purpose. The lines must be thick and the hooks large; for bait we use dragon worms, and we hang a stone or piece of lead the size of a chestnut from the hook so that the line will sink down deep into the pool. No matter how lightly a fish bites on the taut line, the rod will immediately pass the sensation on to the hand, so, rather than watching for a fish, the fisher must feel with his hands and pull the hook up with a jerk the instant the thought "It's biting!" passes through his mind. The rather heavy and struggling creature that emerges is usually a catfish, an eel, or a mandarin fish, or sometimes even a carp, but just occasionally a snake pops up, in which case throw the rod down quickly! Because the rod makes a splashing noise each time it is lowered into the water, this kind of fishing is known as splashing. It does not feel particularly pure or clean, but has something of the pleasure of listening to ghost stories when sitting in a wood lit by fireflies.

Sinking

Sinking refers to regular fishing with a long rod and a fine line, where we set up in one place, sink the rod, and wait for the fish to approach. The bait differs according to the water. If the water is cloudy and there may be carp around, we use worms, but if the water is clear and there is a possibility of finding goby minnow, brook perch, or barbs, then we also use watery bait, shrimp, or soy paste maggots. If the water is fairly deep, but the fish are not gathering in any one particular place where the hook might be sunk, then we have to create such a place. First, we look for a spot where the water seems still and deep enough to reach up to about chest height. Then we wade in and feel with our feet for a space about six feet wide on the riverbed. After pushing any stones out of the way so that there is only soft sand remaining, we dig out a small hole in the center. Then we come back out of the water, gather a large fistful of mud and sesame dregs, and drop it into the center of the hole. Once it has settled, we press it down hard into the sandy bed with our feet and come out of the water again. With such a cozy, soft bed and the smell of sesame wafting around, all kinds of visitors will soon arrive. In some instances, they will just eat the sesame and not bite on the bait, in which case we move onto another place for the day and return to the original spot on the following day, by which time it will be positively bustling with visitors. The sensation of a light pull on the bronze hook, hanging from a float made of kaoliang stalks, the immediate leap in the heart, and the jadelike fish flipping around at the end of the line once the hook has gone down . . . this is the stuff of pleasant tales to be retold the whole summer. Even if the hook never even so much as quivers, it is still quite nice to listen to the song of the cicadas in the hill across the way and think of the one for whom we yearn, left behind in the city.

Playing in the Rapids

Playing in the rapids is a kind of fishing we enjoy during the rainy season, when the water is beginning to drop once more but the current is still swollen to about 50 percent more than its normal height. We move about the shallows with a rod and catch fish such as catfish and minnows. The rod should be light, the line thin, and the hook small. Flies are the best bait.

Playing in the rapids provides the subtlest pleasures of any kind of fishing. First of all, the surrounding landscape actually changes as we move downstream with the water. Then how magical it is to come across the sparkle of a large mouth and tiny scales in shallow water that seems empty of fish. Ripples kick up to the surface, and finally a fish is pulled out of the water. Life flows at length, just like that water we follow between the green mountains on a summer's day, so, when we feel the sensation of lively resilience from silver scales jumping at the end of a fine thread, it is as if we have entered an enchanted land.

Oriental Painting

I am a little dissatisfied that people in the East are more drawn to painting in the Western style than in the Oriental style. If I could only hang a single painting in my home, it would have to be an Oriental one. It is not as if they are so rare that they are hard to find. Recent works by our Oriental-style painters, however, seem like sketches, so far removed are they from art. Anyone who knows even a little about the fine arts, takes pride in himself as an artist, and thinks about self-expression almost certainly paints in the Western style. I wish that painters with such creative powers would show an interest in Oriental painting. To make my position clear, it is as follows:

1. They say that the fine arts, like dance and music, have no national boundaries, but ultimately this is not true. When we look toward the east and west of the oceans, the boundary seems to be especially clear. Not only does Ch'oe Sŭnghŭi make Korean dance seem easy, but no matter how much Chaliapin practiced he would not be able to match Yi Tongbaek with his folktunes.* I do believe that all fine arts present some kind of national boundary, though the degree to which this is so certainly varies. There is no need to even question the fact that for Koreans it was easier to become a Tanwŏn or an Owŏn than a Cezanne or a Matisse.† There has to be some reason to abandon what is easy in favor of something that takes far more effort. Call me a simpleton, but I cannot seem to come up with any such reason. If someone says, "I hate the masters. I paint in the Western style simply because I prefer it," this is perhaps a matter of personal taste and not something a third party should comment upon, and yet, though it may be rude of me, I am going to be a little dogmatic here. Those who prefer Oriental to Western-style painting are more cultured people. I am saying this in defense of Oriental painting rather than in praise of those people, but I admit it smacks of an outrageous dogmatism. How can those who argue that West-

---

* Ch'oe Sŭnghŭi (1911–?) was a world-famous dancer who performed throughout Europe and North and South America during the colonial period. She was especially popular in Japan. After liberation, she moved to North Korea where she continued to dance. Feodor Chaliapin (1873–1938) was one of the greatest Russian opera singers of all times and sang in the most prestigious Western opera houses of the early twentieth century. Yi Tongbaek (1867–1950) was a well-known *p'ansori* singer.

† Tanwŏn is Kim Hongdo (1745–?), one of Korea's best-loved painters. Famous for his genre paintings of scenes from everyday life, Kim Hongdo also painted official receptions, Daoist and Buddhist figures, and landscapes of Korean scenes. Owŏn is Chang Sŭngŏp (1843–1897), who is considered one of the Chosŏn dynasty's three greatest painters, along with Kim Hongdo and An Kyŏn. Chang was known for his drinking and free spirit.

ern painting seems more alive—not on the basis of well-painted nudes but because of principles of color—fail to appreciate the Sŏn, which is the highest expression of cultivation in the Orient?

2. When Orientals paint in the Western style it seems ill-suited to their environment. This is true from an economic point of view, but is it not also true of the subject matter itself? If we look at our natural surroundings, they simply do not resemble those found in Western paintings. In photographs of several famous Western paintings, we find naked bodies either sitting or lying down in grassy fields or on mountain slopes. Try doing that in Korea and the first thing we would have to worry about is being scratched by thorns and the like! We encounter a similar problem when painting the human body. Do not the muscles of Korean women look much less solid than those of Western women? And is not that lack of solidity actually what makes Oriental women so beautiful? One would imagine that just as the human body in the West well suits Western painting then so does the character of its natural surroundings.

3. One has to know how to agonize over one's own contradictions. It is preferable for the artwork and daily life to come together as one. I rarely see anyone in Korea painting in the Western style who actually enjoys the kind of lifestyle that produces Western-style paintings. Producing an artwork in which one cannot oneself live—if that is not a dream then is it not mere labor? Such thoughts are truly depressing.

4. Orientals must take on the mantle of Tanwŏn and Owŏn, and within the Orient Koreans especially should do their part. This is not merely reasonable but also our common desire. Westerners live far away and do not attempt to become the ancestors of Tanwŏn. It would be as difficult for them as it is for a Korean painter to become a second Cezanne. Compared to Korean literature, does not Korean art also have a much richer heritage? Whence comes the need to leave that heritage to rot in order to gaze at the Eiffel Tower on some distant horizon?

For these reasons I am foolish enough to hope that a vigorous campaign will come about advocating a renaissance in Korean painting through a transition away from the Western style and back toward the Oriental style.

I would like to address a word here to those who are already painting in the Oriental style. Several years ago I heard that there was to be a show by a great artist and went to take a look. An album was on display that seemed out of place on such an occasion; it was a scrapbook of reviews and comments advertising the works. I was more than a little annoyed. Had not the artist heard the anecdote of Tanwŏn, who would give two hundred *nyang* for one vase of plum blossom, even though he could not afford to buy rice or salt, or of Owŏn, who sent only an eight-piece folding screen to the king, when twelve pieces had been asked for, and ran away when summoned back to the palace? The greatness of Oriental painting is to be found in its spirit, not in its handicraft.

Antiques

Our elders do not always brandish their authority. Sometimes a quiet withdrawal to the lowest seat can be a beautiful form of humility.

There is no elder in our home. Sometimes I become arrogant. The only thing older than me is the water dropper that my father once used. I only have to gaze at it in a quiet place and think that it was once used by my father, and a scene of which I have only heard, of my father who enjoyed calligraphy, permeates the room along with the fragrance of ink. Adjusting his sleeves to sit in quiet contemplation is a true lesson that my father passed on by example.

I inherited this object, which suffered tribulations together with my father for I do not know how long. Although I was young when I saw that water dropper at my father's bedside along with several brushes, the memory is by no means faint: the life of an exile with no promise of a land in which his body might be buried, those winter nights in Vladivostok where even the sea would freeze and the sound of the waves fall silent, and then my father's passing away, his heart still gripped by resentment and regret. This was the water dropper that my maternal grandmother had always carried in her waistband, waiting for me to grow up, saying this is something your father once used. It was fired at the royal kilns and shaped like a heavenly peach—a light blue body with red spots.

Of course this one item of stationery belonging to my late father is hardly the only thing to have suffered together with men of old. I have gradually come to respect the objects belonging to earlier generations. From time to time I recall a phrase from a Whitman poem, which reads "Oh, beautiful woman, old woman!" But when I think of the everyday grime of past people's lives, which had seeped and spread into each crack and broken rim of perhaps their only teacup or wine jar, it is not an old woman's wrinkles that come to mind, but rather the beautiful colors of twilight.

Chosŏn period porcelain, no less than Koryŏ porcelain, is gradually making a favorable impression among pot lovers around the world. Yi dynasty vessels in particular were not developed as commodities, unlike those of China or the Japanese metropole, and so although the hands of the craftsmen were expert, their hearts were as pure as children. Pots made by experienced hands with hearts lacking in worldly desire are closer to nature than to artifice. These pots may not catch the eye at first glance, but the eye never tires of looking at them, and so an attachment is formed. Once our troubled eyes or hearts reach there and find comfort in the absence of words, we begin to think of the distant past, which appears immense, but there is no sense of suffocation, only a pure heart remaining.

When Li Bai climbed the mountain of Jingting, he recited the following poem:

The myriad birds high in the sky have flown away;
A lone cloud floats leisurely by.
We look and neither of us grows tired,
That can only be the Jingting Mountain.

When my twittering children have all fallen asleep, and even my wife has retired to her bed like a lonely cloud, that is when we look and neither of us grows tired; at one with these antiques, I am unaware of the deepening night.

It is not enough to value them for their age or to appreciate them solely for the technique and vigor with which they were made. What makes old things seem old are the traces they hold of having lived together with the people of the past. Foreign arts and crafts are so ornate that with just one little crack they are already rendered useless. Like people who wear silk clothes and yet have rough hands and feet, the more the traces of life remain the less beautiful such objects seem. However, our Chosŏn period arts and crafts are so simple in their nature that they grow ever more beautiful as they soak up dirt and food. This is not only the case for porcelain. Woodwork is like this too. Pillows, clogs, dishes—all enter our lives and tend to become more beautiful the more they soak up the grime of their users. Although of late Western books suffer the fate of becoming only more dirty and ugly from the day they are bought, our Korean books have to soak up a certain amount of dirt in order that their covers shine and their pages turn smoothly. A few days ago, by chance I acquired the *Letters* of the Enlightened Teacher Dahui.* The edition goes back more than four hundred years, to the time of the Jiajing emperor,†

---

* Dahui (1089–1163) was a Chinese Chan master known for his advocacy of the use of koans in daily meditation as a way to achieve enlightenment open to all.

† Jiajing is the reign name for the Ming emperor Shizong, who reigned from 1521–1566.

and used to belong to Ch'usa Kim Chŏnghŭi, whom I hold in the highest reverence. His seal is affixed, particles have been added throughout the volume, and there are even annotations in places, although I do not know whether they are his. *Letters* is such a difficult text that I can barely understand even one line properly, yet I only have to hold it for a while and look at its cover, with the title standing there unchanged for so many years, or open the pages and see the traces where our ancestors read, or think of how this one volume was created over several months or years, as stroke by stroke each character was written and then carved out in rows, before I feel a kind of contrition at how today, thanks to print, we so discourteously publish all kinds of writing in haste, whether well written or badly composed.

It would be rash to consider the appreciation of antiques to be a pastime of the rich or the hermit alone. To satisfy one's acquisitive desires with money is merely to seek entertainment, and to desire that which lies beyond one's reach is vanity itself. The appreciation and enjoyment of things as a professional activity, rather than a mere hobby, has little to do with either idleness or vanity.

Antiques and Daily Life

When objects are no longer of any use, we usually refer to them as *koltongp'um*, "antiques." This playful manner of speaking is not only used to refer to objects but to people as well. We jokingly refer to those old-fashioned people, who appear to exist at a remove from the present, as antiques. *Koltong* is used as a substitute for "useless" or "worthless." Sometimes this substitution is extended in meaning to refer not just to the antiques themselves but also to those lovers of the past who treasure antiques. The somewhat groundless expression arises from the idea that those who collect antiques are useless and worthless people in reality.

Of course, the two characters for *koltong*, 骨董, meaning "bone" and "to lead someone the correct way," are Chinese. The characters *kodong*, 古董, meaning "old" and "to lead someone the correct way," are also used; in fact these characters are used as phonetic replacements for *kodong*, 古銅, "old bronze." That bad habit we see in Chinese writing, of casually substituting the proper characters with homophonic characters of a different meaning, reached as far as this "old bronze" too. But whereas *old* is a character with a profound reverberation that those such as Ch'usa wrote with great pleasure, *bone* is a character that one might pick out in a crematorium, a character suggesting a gaunt death! Think how much life is stripped from these antiques when they are referred to using this character for bone. As language is the possession of the masses, we cannot correct it just as we please, but when possible I choose to refer to antiques as *kowanp'um*, 古翫品, "old playthings."

Recently, even young people are becoming sick of the "new style." We see this same passion for the classics in antique shops too. Even four or five years ago it would have been hard to meet someone young in an antique store. There were mostly old men who would upon entry remove from their head a faded fedora, which looked as if it had been worn for a century or more, and then would bend over, taking out their spectacles in order to examine the objects. Nowadays, it is not so difficult to meet those same young gentlemen we once saw in Western goods stores in antique stores instead. This is a positive development that is breathing fresh air into our antique stores.

It is not as if the daily lives of old men are essentially morbid, but for some reason I cannot help but taste the gloom of buying funeral cloth whenever I see an old man buying old objects.

Nevertheless we must reflect upon how young people literally lose themselves in play. Perhaps there is a necessity to keep watch on young men in sofar as antiques are concerned, especially for we Orientals who are already aging too soon in so many other respects. When we talk about Korean antiques, we are generally talking, aside from calligraphy, about pottery and especially Yi porcelain. With the exception of some small items of stationery, these are women's toilet accessories and kitchen utensils. Teabowls and wine jars are, of course, also kitchen utensils. However, some lovers of old things have much more than stationery items in their rooms. Plates that used to hold greens or leftovers are hung on the wall and jars that once held grain syrup and flour are arranged respectably in front of famous works of calligraphy and paintings. Things like powder cases, salt bowls, or spoon and chopstick holders are resurrected as ink pad cases, dishes for washing brushes, and ashtrays. No one feels the need to delve into their origins or the class of their owners to see what use they once served. Perhaps compressing our current lives into these vessels, which supported our ancestors' lives for so long, is the proper interpretation of the classics or tradition after all. But it does seem awfully easy for *yangban* to fall into a narrow and timid way of life as they pick and choose from women's kitchen utensils and arrange them in their rooms. They must look quite petty to the adventurers of the world. It is easy to fall utterly and completely under the charm of "pouring drinks and writing poems for each other, or taking solitary pleasure from planting flowers and moving stones." We are able to easily shut ourselves up for several days enjoying the hanging of a picture anew or changing the place of one empty dish. We become immersed in stillness and a sense of proximity. It is because of this that the extreme short-sighted nature of antiquarians is apt to form. It is an empty dish and empty vase. It does not contain rice cakes or water, but silence and emptiness. Already it is no longer a vessel but a world, a universe. To someone else it may look no more than a fragment of porcelain, but to its owner it is an endless landscape and a sublime temple. This is the extreme realm of the antique, but the owner must realize that this is also the realm where he himself is taken prisoner as a useless human being.

For young people to lose the "present" is not the same as old people's inability to monopolize the realm of the antique.

Rare books bring honor to old scholars simply by virtue of being in their collection. However, let us say that a young scholar takes possession of a rare book of his dreams, such as the *Items from the Three Eras of Silla*.* If all he does is add it to his collection, then where is the honor? Of course, to keep something as a mere antique is not the worst kind of hobby. But if collecting is his only business, that falls into the realm of greed. For without some degree of research or criticism, appreciation also becomes less a case of licking the surface of a watermelon than being drawn toward a base attraction without discovering the true meaning of the old vessel. Furthermore, if one's own spirit actually becomes depressed, this can cause no small amount of damage.

If we stop only at the point of preserving the classics or tradition, then that is death: it is digging a grave. There is no reason for us to use time and money in order to turn our studies into graves.

When young intellectuals acquire pottery, they should do so with the same purpose as when they collect old books. They should not stop at appreciation or the desire to possess, but discover their proper modern interpretation as a work of art or craft. We must shake the dust of death from the old object and help turn it into a phoenix of new beauty and life. That is the point where I believe the antique can truly be brought into our daily lives.

---

* *Samdaemok*: the first recorded collection of Korean poetry, put together in 888. It is no longer extant.

Fiction

This happened some years ago. I met the father of one of my friends from the countryside for the first time in several years.

"They say that you're making quite a name for yourself recently with your writing. What kind of writing is it that you do?"

When I hesitated, not knowing how to answer, his son answered in my place,

"It's called fiction. They say he writes pretty interesting stuff."

A frown passed over the old man's brow, as if this was unexpected,

"Fiction? You mean those storybooks?"

He asked, and I replied,

"That's right."

He was a little flustered,

"Well, what do you do that for? From old, fiction meant those common stories collected by low-rank officials. Nothing more than market gossip . . . "

At this, I felt rather cowed and was grateful to be able to think of writers such as Tolstoy.

I might have been thoroughly disheartened had I not at that moment suddenly recalled once seeing Tolstoy and Hugo's photographs among those of other great people in a picture postcard store.

I realized just how truly thankful I am to those early translators who brought us the literature of the West. For it was in the West that fiction was transformed into literature for the first time.

If those Western novels had not usurped the throne of literature, I wonder how many writers in the East, and especially in places like Korea, would have been happy to find their vocation in writing those stories despised by so many as market gossip.

I have always felt more than a little displeased with terms such as *market gossip* or *tales of the street and alley.* Why must fiction necessarily concern itself with clouds of dust, spattering spit, bloody smells, and screams? To the extent possible I have tried to write in a way that avoids the dust and the spit and eschews bloody smells and screams. Perhaps this stems from a slight lack of awareness regarding "fiction," which itself arises from my resistance to the way fiction is considered vulgar. It was in those remote classics written in Chinese that they coined the terms *market gossip* and *tales of the street and alley*. Yet how clearly they understood the nature of fiction already! Fiction does not progress; today's fiction has not departed one bit from the definition that was bequeathed by Chinese writings. That market gossip would best equate to the newspapers in recent times. It is, in fact, the newspaper of humanity, edited effectively and with one goal in mind. Its sensibility and style are good, along with its intellect and appearance, but in the end do such things amount to anything more than the nervous exhaustion of pale young prose writers trying to enhance themselves? "A record of the most energetic attachment, without a moment of rest, to the various phenomena of the current world"—a ceaselessly flowing human river in writing—it is here where the real identity and dignity of prose and thus fiction lies. With fiction, the first question must be not "who wrote" but "who read." Perhaps the main thing that today's writers need to reflect upon is their weak vision and, to borrow a classical idiom, the way in which in their attempts to craft prose they "fall into stupidity as they strive for refinement." I write these words more to myself than to anyone else.

Recently, Chinese characters have begun to appear in fictional sentences. This is an unfortunate development for the true nature of "market gossip." I myself experimented with using Chinese characters some years ago in a short piece titled "Old Man Uam." It is a most effective way of evoking the flavor of the *sasosŏl* and the air of the anecdotal essay. But, in their turn, abuses soon arise. In order to try to protect the harmony of phrases in which Chinese characters appear, I try hard to use less onomatopoeia and those words that mimic behavior. But where does that leave people like us who use such words so precisely and abundantly in our every-day spoken language?

> She Wrapped a Red Ribbon beneath her Radiant hair, Pinched a Pearly right cheek, and bit down on her lips . . .
>
> *[From Yŏm Sangsŏp's "Telephone"]**

> Whoosh whoosh, a stream rushes by, splash splash, another stream over there; streams from all ten valleys collide into one, and, helter-skelter, leaping up, spraying out, dangling tendrils down, dripping . . . waves crash, splash, and rumble into the folding-screen rock over there . . .
>
> *[From "The Picnic Song"]*†

Such passages, almost entirely free from any Chinese words as they are, reveal a tenacious energy rather than being what we might call concrete. How could one take clay that is so delightfully sticky for sculpting a world of prose and think it strange enough to need sand added for refinement? In other forms of writing, it is fine to enjoy the fun of Chinese characters, but in fiction and "tales of the street and alleys," which offer few rewards for such effort, is it not better to be wary of possible failure in advance when forcing the conceptualization of one's self-expression?

It is not necessarily good for students to read fiction. This is because they might become so absorbed in it that they pay insufficient attention to their other studies. Of course it is fine if they

---

* "Telephone" was a short story written in 1925 by Yŏm Sangsŏp, one of the pioneers of modern Korean literature.

† The Picnic Song or "Yusan'ga" was known as one of the "twelve songs" that were popular with singers and storytellers from the middle of the nineteenth century.

read fiction while also paying due attention to those other studies. In fact, I would say that we should encourage them to do so. To know nothing of the way of the world or human emotions is not naïveté, but stupidity. There are many educators who do not know the difference between stupidity and naïveté and who openly express disdain if you even mention the word *fiction*. They are those musty Confucian scholars who lecture that the *Essentials of Enlightenment* constitutes true literature.* Their extreme emphasis on sobriety, both at home and at school, is their only weapon to try to hide their own ignorance and sloth, rather than to protect their students as they proclaim. In the East still today, regardless of how society has advanced, these narrow-minded dullards have in their ignorance trampled all over the gardens of our young people's emotions!

Greetings

This happened back in the countryside when I was still in middle school. I had gone to pay my respects to a certain old man. He sat on the wooden bed near the fireplace, holding a fan in one hand and fingering his beard with the other. I bowed quietly on the spot where I stood just outside the sliding door. And then I retreated without saying a word.

The next day I saw the old man in his yard.

"When did you get here?"

"Yesterday, sir."

"You rascal, and you didn't come and say hello . . . "

---

* The *Essentials of Enlightenment* (Kyŏngmong yogyŏl) is a textbook written in 1575 by the Confucian scholar Yulgok Yi I (1536–1584).

I received a mild scolding. On the previous day that old man must have been looking down, absorbed in his thoughts.

Once in the past, a country gentleman visited the Taewŏn'gun and bowed outside the sliding door in the upper room.* When the gentleman looked up, the Taewŏn'gun was still leaning silently on a cushion, looking down at a book. The gentleman thought the Taewŏn'gun must not have seen and so he bowed again. At which the Taewŏn'gun suddenly shouted so loud that the gentleman jumped with shock.

"What kind of outrageous act is this? Bowing twice to a living person, do you think I am a corpse?"

The gentleman replied deftly and quickly,

"Oh no, sir, the first was a bow of greeting, and the second a bow of farewell."

The Taewŏn'gun nodded with delight to have found such a good man.

Apparently it could sometimes be polite to be impolite. If it was a cold day and one saw an elder coming from the opposite direction, one was supposed to quickly hide in a side alley. This was not because it is troublesome to bow respectfully, but because it would force the elder to remain longer in the cold in order to receive such a greeting. What if he were to even stop and talk in the cold wind? How indebted one would be for the trouble caused! This was the extremity of etiquette.

They say that Chŏng Widang was once passing through Namdaemun Street when he encountered a certain old man; he placed

---

* The Taewŏn'gun (1820–1898) was the father of King Kojong (r. 1864–1907) and ruled Korea as de facto regent during the late 1860s, passing through a popular reform program. Although forced to retire to the country-side for his contemptuous treatment of Queen Min, his daughter-in-law, the Taewŏn'gun never fully gave up his political activities.

the book he was carrying down on the road and quickly knelt down to bow in the slippery earth that had once been frozen but was now in the process of melting.* Later, when questioned by his companion, Chŏng replied that the old man had been his teacher. That was not so long ago. Now, if we were to see such a scene in front of these buildings where the cars race by, it would be more miraculous than picking up a piece of Koryŏ celadon in the street!

In recent years, the forms of greeting that we regularly exchange have degraded to a most deplorable extent. At a distance of three to four steps, our hand reaches to our hat. The movement could not even definitively be described as *seeming* to remove one's hat, let alone actually removing it. While pretending to finger one part of our hat within easy reach, we draw closer and move quickly to grasp the other person's hand. From time to time I reflect upon this habit of shaking hands and realize that there is no real standard. It is quite similar to the way we put our hands to our hats. The one hand does not even race with confidence toward the other. It might not even feel the need for a handshake depending upon the degree of intimacy. Often both parties are taken by surprise and simply pass each other by discretely, or else one side goes so far as to reach out a startled hand while the other side begins his preparations only upon hearing the words "So how have you been?" But it is not until he looks down by chance and sees the outstretched hand that he finally grasps it with an exclamation of "Ah!" He might then shake it with renewed effort or, if he is not alert or had been walking along engrossed in his own thoughts, he might even just pass by, although he has clearly seen this hand reaching out, or he might hold out his hand too late,

---

* Widang is the pen name of Chŏng Inbo (1892–ca. 1950), a respected Confucian historian and scholar of Chinese during the colonial period.

when the first hand is already withdrawing, and barely manage to shake one finger. The funniest handshake is when one side is so slow to reach out that not even a finger ends up being grasped and so both hands are held out and then dropped, having merely signified an intention.

Done properly, the handshake is of all greetings a good one, which gives a sense of a person's "real feelings." Even a blind person would be able to recognize Mongyang from his handshake.* Then, in complete contrast to his strong will, there is the characteristic passivity of someone like Minch'on, who would also easily disclose himself to a blind person.†

At any rate, it seems to me that the individuality of the handshake and the lack of individuality of the bow sufficiently suggest the difference between Eastern and Western cultures.

I recall a fascinating passage about hands from an essay by that great Swiss scholar Harudi, which I will translate roughly here:‡

A person's hands are the best way to get to know someone. There is the hand of the serious man that reaches out with self-respect, the slippery outstretched hand of the lady socialite, the hand of the insincere egoist who considers important the mere

---

* Mongyang is the pen name of Yŏ Unhyŏng (1886–1947), a political activist and newspaper editor. He was a member of the Provisional Government in Exile in Shanghai, attended the drafting of the Declaration of Independence in 1919, became leader of the Korean Workers' Party, and, after liberation, the Korean People's Party before his assassination in 1947.

† Minch'on is the pen name of Yi Kiyŏng (1895–1984), a novelist and member of KAPF. Probably the most well-respected leftist novelist in both South and North Korea (where he later lived) and author of the canonical novel of peasant life *Kohyang* (Native land; 1934).

‡ It is unclear who this Swiss scholar is, whose name is rendered in *han'gŭl* as Harudi.

holding out of the hand, the cold and clammy hand of the man on the verge of a nervous breakdown, the decorated hand of the person who is lazy at work, and the hand that is rough from hard labor. All these hands reveal themselves more truly than does the mouth or even our eyes. One of the most delightful things is a child's hand, which reaches out eagerly, full of a trust that comes from deep within an innocent heart. This hand, just like an animal's paw, is also a perfect symbol of intimacy. In contrast, if the hand gesture is frivolously affected, if the arms are completely spread open, or if the handshake lacks decorum, if two hands are held out at once, if the hand is shaken with a fuss or is grasped for too long and not let go, this always leaves a suspicion on the other side that there might be the intention of trying to leave a certain impression.

The Old Writings of Two Qing Poets

A long time ago, a man named Kuo took some of his poems to Wandang and asked for a title upon which to compose more poems. It appears that in Wandang's title were included the words "Make the two poets Feng and Li the focus of your efforts." He was referring to Yushan Feng Minchang and Erjiao Li Jian, both new poets of the Qing dynasty who would not have been well known among the Yi dynasty literati, immersed as they were solely in the poets of the Tang and Song dynasties. Kuo was unable to find the writings of Feng and Li, and so he visited Wandang again, upon which Wandang gave him a handwritten booklet about Feng and Li. It included the following appendix:

There is no document in my bundle to bear witness to the old writings of the two poets, but there is this small book recorded by hand. With this fallen feather and piece of a scale perhaps it is possible to trace their origins back to the larger kingfisher and whale.

Fortunately, this booklet has been passed down to us intact today, and it includes twenty poems by Yushan written in honor of Du Shaoling and another twenty written in honor of Han Wengong.* For Erjiao, it includes his writing on poetry rather than his actual poems. His brilliant, unrestrained spirit seems certainly to have been a major source for Wandang himself. These writings on poetry alone are sufficient to constitute a major piece of art theory, not merely from the Qing and Yi dynasties, but from all times spanning East and West. Allow me to introduce it here:

> The gentleman-scholar is born in the wake of his ancestors,
> so how could he not follow in their footsteps?
> At first, he masters all the schools,
> and finally he raises his own spear.
> He serves in a regiment and becomes a great leader.
> With a commanding voice, he orders his soldiers to attack
>   great enemies.
> In his one life he suffers many lives and deaths,
> and with his learning as a resource, he survives a hundred
>   battles.
> When he reaches the precipice, there is no more easy step,
> so he raises his voice to a higher pitch and the flute, too,
>   breaks;
> He draws an arrow and stone seems to turn to flesh;
> he sharpens his sword but the water is already red.

---

* Also known as the great Tang poet Du Fu (712–770) and essayist and poet Han Yu (768–824) respectively.

What is essential starts with the beginnings,
though his true spirit will leap up and penetrate the rainbow.*

And finally,

> People of the world look at me, but I shut the door tightly.
> The vines of ivy reach dark and deep, while white clouds float
>   outside my door.
> The lonely night is long, and I caress my zither.
> Who will hear this tune? What I cherish is my own
>   heart.

After this short verse, Wandang, who even took "A man of sorrow" as his nom de plume, added a short verse beneath the phrase "What I cherish is my own heart," writing in especially tiny characters, "The four characters, 'what I cherish is my own heart,' explain the hearts of writers since ancient times." Have writers' hearts really been like this since of old?

Furthermore, after each selection of writing, Wandang has written his own comments upon the personal character of the poet and his works. These are worth considering for many reasons. I record briefly just some important parts here:

> Feng Yushan . . . when he was a young man he took as his teacher the Old Master Beiping, and was praised by him greatly. After following his guidance for a long time, Feng's knowledge was deep. Whenever mention was made of the

---

* This refers to Mencius's idea that man's innate goodness is comprised of the "four beginnings": commiseration, shame, courtesy, and the ability to tell right from wrong.

Old Master, Feng would immediately bow his head in respect, and when he spoke of his teacher's instruction, he
would never tire of repeating it. When he paid his respects to
his grandfather on the first day of each month, he would follow the exact same protocol with his teacher from beginning
to end. . . . Li Erjiao . . . his poetry begins with Shangu and
then moves into Du Fu. He has drawn discipline from Daxie, strength from Changli, profundity from Changji, beauty
from Yuqi, a certain leanness from Dongye, and eccentricity
from Langxian.*

Whenever his teacher's name was mentioned, he bowed his
head in respect, and on the first of each month he paid respects to
his teacher along with his grandfather. This is beautiful virtue on a
par with the moral laws of the universe.

Are we not equally surprised by Wandang's magnanimous yet
delicate poetic eye? A great writer does not lose his critical eye
when choosing his intimate friends.

---

* Shangu is also known as Huang Tingjian (1045–1105), one of the best-
known calligraphers and poets of the Northern Song dynasty; Daxie is Xie
Lingyun (385–433), one of the foremost poets of the Southern and Northern
dynasties; Changli is influential essayist and poet Han Yu (768–824) of
the Tang dynasty; Changji is Li He (790/1–816), a talented poet considered
imaginative but unconventional; Yuqi is Li Shangyin (ca. 810s–858), a sen-
suous poet who was "rediscovered" in the twentieth century; Dongye is
Meng Dongye (751–814), a Tang poet who, along with Han Yu, is known for
his attempt to write in the ancient style; and Langxian is the poet Jia Dao
(779–843).

Diary from a Seaside Village (Shōwa 11)

July 2 (Thursday)

At five o'clock on a drizzly morning in Anbyŏn, we disembarked from the train headed for Ch'ŏngjin when, with no time even for a glance around, the train for Kansŏng pulled in.

Hemp-skirted women with white cotton towels tied around their heads stepped on and off, chatting in Wŏnsan accents. Old grandmothers carried wooden bowls stained with fish scales; from their conversations wafted the smell of freshly gathered oysters. A couple of stations later the ocean appeared. The ocean! I wanted to clap my hands. The East Sea was stained a deep indigo, but in the mist it seemed as dim as a dream. Our train skirted around the sea as if avoiding a picture being painted. Here and there sandy beaches entreated us to stop and walk upon them. Fishermen wearing raincoats, in groups of ten or more, hauled in their fishnets. What kind of fish? But our train passed by such scenes.

Last summer I had actually come as far as Songjŏn for a short while. As Usan had told me it would be convenient to stay in Kojŏ, I then left Songjŏn behind, but any affection I might have had for Kojŏ vanished the instant I laid my eyes on it. I felt as if I were in the bottom of a storehouse, which is exactly what the characters for *kojŏ* mean. All the roofs were made of galvanized iron, the earth was dark, the sea was faraway, and even Ch'ongsŏk Pavilion looked to be at least ten *li* from there. The inn had electricity and a telephone so I suppose one could call it convenient, just as Usan had said, but it did not possess even a smattering of character. Give me any day the cozy lodging at a village inn from which emanates the smell of cloth leggings belonging to those traveling by foot. This place was half Japanese, and so it had *fusuma* quilts spread out on paper-covered floors. Worst of all, the floors in the corridor were so thin that each time rubber slippers flipped past I leaped with surprise. I could not get any sleep at all. And why were all the electric lights hanging from the ceiling as if this were some kind of cell?

In the evening the lights came on, and it grew a little cozier. I forced myself to change my mood and pick up my pen.

I had been determined to write at least one episode of my novel before I went to bed, but just then a gramophone was turned on in the room next door. It appeared that the Japanese language teacher from the local school boarded here.

When he called the servant boy, he pronounced the three characters of his name with a precise Japanese accent, as if he were calling on a pupil in his classroom. Then the gramophone began to play a popular jazz song, "*Uta wa kikumono, odori wa mirumono . . .* Songs are to be heard, and dance to be seen . . . " From rooms here and there people gathered, greeting him respectfully in Japanese, "Good evening, teacher."

Anger welled up inside me, but after a while even that awful row seemed to gradually improve, like swallowing a cheap ice cream with no thought of spitting it out.

I never set eyes on that *sensei*, but he must have left his hometown some thousands of *li* away to come to this remote place, only to be harassed by his students all day long. When I thought of him seeking some consolation in his exhausting life with a few popular songs of an evening, I almost shed a few tears on his behalf.

Even if I could not write the daily installment of my novel, I decided to first write this at least.

July 3 (Friday)

I decide to leave Ch'ongsŏk Pavilion for tomorrow and go to Songjŏn.

I wonder why a place as nice as Songjŏn is not more well known, and why it does not have a nice clean inn or a villa to rent. There are only two inns, both no more than lodges: one of them has no name, and the other has a large sign reading "East Sea Inn." I opt for the one with the name.

Just as Kojŏ is like the floor of a storehouse, Songjŏn is like the field of pine trees that comprise its characters. The village, too, is half buried in pine trees. As the trees have grown up in ocean winds, they have thick trunks but few branches; they all lean over backward and are of quite the most fashionable shape, almost like parasols. If one were to spread out a mat underneath, each pine tree would make a fine pavilion.

I only have to look at the pine trees and it feels like spring. They are not merely green but positively shimmering. If I look at the earth, then it feels like autumn. The sand is soft and so blindingly bright I can almost hear it crackling.

The path from the village to the sea is good. Such wide paths with pine trees lining both sides can be found in many places, and not just Songjŏn to be sure. But I have rarely walked down a path as clean and pretty as this one. It is the kind of path that a new bride and groom should walk down after coming out of the ceremony hall. At the end of the path there is open sky and wide ocean, and stretching out firmly into the air is something so unexpected I feel as though I have entered a surrealist painting—an iron bar that has harmonized with the scenery. I run toward it, hoist myself up, and just about manage four chin-ups.

The ocean waves are rough: a misty ocean spray covers the coast like a snowstorm. Here and there rugosa roses flutter in the wind, as if trying not to be forgotten. Their fragrance is strong but, buried by the scent of the waves, it only reaches the nostrils if one breaks off a bloom. The ocean always appears to be young.

My window was so bright at night that I mentioned it to the owner, who told me it was because of the full moon. It was cool enough to feel chilly in my thin summer jacket, but I stepped out of the inn once again.

On the path that had been so empty during the daytime there was not even the trace of a human shadow at night. Instead it was full of the moonlight. With each step I advanced, the waves from the moon seem to scatter in splashes. A vast ocean belonging to the moon lay over the path, over the pinewoods, the railway tracks and the majestic ocean itself. Oh, how small the watery waves appear beneath this ocean of the moon!

This lunar ocean is sacred!

For whom does the moon shine so bright, when there is not a single bird singing in the pine trees and only empty villas with tightly shut windows? Whether people come outside to gaze upon it or not, the moon shines brilliantly even here, where there is no still water that might capture its reflection but only the crashing waves. I wonder in how many unpopulated places and how far and wide this moon shines? In the endless desert, over the endless ocean, and on each deserted island, on the highest peaks, the polar regions of the north and south, and even on the worlds belonging to each of those countless stars hanging in space, the moon is terrifyingly large and lacking in worldly desire! As a human being of no account, I would gladly give all my affection to the moon!

July 4 (Saturday)

The morning is dazzling.

The sky looks as if it might crackle like fresh wrapping paper.

Directly in front of my room lies the unfenced sports ground belonging to the local normal school. At the sound of the school bell, I too went outside. I walked into the pine trees to the side of the ground and observed the morning assembly.

After each class leader had stepped forward and herded the students into lines, the oldest-looking teacher, who must have been the headmaster, stood up on a platform about half a man's length.

Then, as if in chorus, what looked like an army of no less than three hundred students all bowed at once with the greeting,

"*Sensei ohayo gozaimasu.* Good morning teacher."

The headmaster put one hand in his trouser pocket and, after clearing his throat, began his official announcements. He told students not to pick fruit from the cherry trees, for not only would they get upset stomachs but what would happen, after all, if they were to fall from the trees as they climbed?

"The cherry is the one fruit that is not for eating," he concluded, and with those words he stood down. Next a teacher wearing a shirt and no jacket quickly jumped up. With no further ado, the whole yard was absorbed in following along with the radio exercises.

I was more than a little pleased. I have already tried three or four times without success to learn these exercises. Even if I manage to follow when someone is showing me, when I try them alone I forget either the movements or the order in which they should be done. As I had been wanting to try some exercise anyway, this was an opportunity not to be missed. I hid behind a pine tree, so that I could see them without being seen myself, and followed along. I do not know how the children could move so quickly, but I was only able to copy about half of each exercise. Still I managed to shuffle through until the end and only then did I look behind me. I had thought that there were only pine trees, but a farmer driving an ox had stopped along his way and stood there watching me. I tried flashing him a smile, but my new friend turned out to be rather rude, for he just spat once and plodded on.

When the bell rang to signal the end of classes, the boys ran out into the front yard and the girls rushed into the back. The girls split once more into groups. The first and second graders scattered randomly to play, whereas the slightly bigger girls, who looked to be in the fifth or sixth grade, gathered their heads together beneath the fence, where they stood whispering, singing, and chattering along happily. A few loners stood to the side sniffling: some just stared at the ground while others would seem suddenly distant and look up at the sky. I wonder what reflections shone in their bright eyes.

Whether it was time for lessons to begin or end, the sound of the waves persisted ever the same.

July 11 (Sunday)

On the way back from a trip to Kaesŏng to see Sŏsa Pavilion, I dropped by my home and brought my family back to Songjŏn with me.

My barefooted kids loved the golden sand that was right outside our front door. I too am all for walking around barefoot.

This was the first time our children had come to the seaside. The smallest, Sonam, jumped about wildly, while Yubaek stood still and stared before wanting to go back to the town because it was too noisy. Only Somyŏng was so busy collecting mussel shells that she did not even think to look at the sea. I guess that our individuality reveals itself most clearly when we are young.

July 14 (Tuesday)

More than anything my wife loved the fact that fish are so plentiful. A string of about twenty leaping flatfish costs forty *chŏn* for big ones only; freshly gathered mussels are eight or nine *chŏn* for a string; a fish called *kkongch'i* that is good salted and broiled costs just ten *chŏn* per string; and then, on the more expensive side, there are sea cucumbers and abalone, which if still alive and kicking begin at fifteen *chŏn* for a string of cucumbers and twenty-five *chŏn* for the abalone. For several days my wife bought more than she had time to eat, tempted by the bargains, but now she seems to be sick of the very smell of fish. Now she says she wants to eat chicken.

In the evening the old lady next-door dropped by with an old hen after we had mentioned we would pay seventy *chŏn*.

"Could you please kill it for us?"

We are all fierce eaters when it comes to chicken, but none of us could have actually cut its throat.

The old lady asked us for a knife and went off to the flax field. However, after a while she still had not returned. We went to find her, thinking that the hen had escaped, but the poor old lady just sat listlessly with tears in her eyes, one hand holding the hen and the other the knife.

"Why are you sitting here instead of killing it?"

"I just don't think I can kill something that I brought up," she said and stood up.

"Then what shall we do?"

"I'll go back home, and when my son comes in the evening I'll get him to do it."

The startled-looking hen was carried back home again, clueless as to what was happening.

July 19 (Sunday)

The weather has been fine for days in a row. The sand is so hot that you cannot walk on it with bare feet. I went down to the sea, and a young boy was fishing in some very shallow water. I wondered what on earth he would catch in such a place, but when I looked again he had caught a fish that was truly beautiful; its scales shone brilliantly and it was really quite large. He told me it was called a yellowtail. I immediately ran home and fetched my fishing rod. I had caught two fish by lunchtime, but mine were both tiny little things the size of fishing floats. Still, it felt satisfying.

July 20 (Monday)

In the morning I forced myself to sit down and write two installments of my novel, and then in the afternoon I went to the sea with
my family. My feet and my back felt as if they were scorching. I have
never jumped into the water in as great a hurry as today. The breeze
was coming from the sultry continent to the west and was as unbearably hot as the air from the heater they use on your hair at the
barber's. As soon as we came out of the water our bodies were dry,
leaving white traces of salt on our shoulders. Our skin began to burn
badly. We headed to Omaeri to watch the fishing boats, which were
clearly visible to the left in the evening sun. The women from the village were waiting for the boats to return, holding bowls of millet and
jars of soy sauce. It looked like a scene from the ancient past. It was
not long before these tiny boats, no bigger than the skiffs on the Tae-
dong River, began to return one by one. The women pushed forward
to meet them. On the fishboats there were just flatfish and sculpins;
the fishermen exchanged fish for goods, counting the fish they put
in the bowls according to the goods they were given in return. On
the clam boats there were mussels, sea cucumbers, and abalone,
and half of these too were exchanged for goods. We bought mussels
and flatfish with money. The fishermen liked our money best.

July 22 (Wednesday)

A fresh breeze is blowing off the ocean and also through the pine
forest.

On the distant, semicircular horizon, a tiny steamboat drags a
thread of smoke behind it. I would like to sail far away. Rolling my
trousers up, I run down to the bottom of Omaeri.

I wrote four installments of my novel and went to Kojŏ to mail
them off. I wish they would open a post office here in Songjŏn and
that I could send registered mail and cash money there too.

There was about five hours left before the return bus would leave for Kojŏ.

I go past the harbor construction and on to Ch'ongsŏk Pavilion.

Once I am past the harbor, the graves appear: graves amidst the sound of the waves and the seagulls, graves looking out onto a vast gulf of water and sky. Even the dirges here seem to be more plaintive.

Pass these graves and the Ch'ongsŏk Pavilion has still to come into sight, but one can begin to sense the rock clusters. The massive, iron-colored crystallized rocks all hold up their heads like fortresses facing enemy ships.

The rocks are hexagonal, whether lying horizontal or standing up. The first couple of these fortressed ridges are lying down, but the rest stand straight up like folding screens and hang out into the water. On the top of the rock formation stands a pavilion, looking as if it might at any moment fly away.

There is no need for a sign to know that this is Ch'ongsŏk Pavilion.

A closer look reveals that these are not cliffs connected like a folding screen but stone pillars standing on slender bases. Much like the columns of Roman ruins, each rock stands by itself in the water. To look down from the height of these stone pillars makes one dizzy: the water below is as dark as poison, leering like a beast of prey. All energy drains from my body in an instant.

Climb up to the pavilion and it is somewhat displeasing to see the calligraphy of Haegang hung on the front, mixed in with praise for the cliffs written by the local school heads.*

---

* Haegang is the pen name of Kim Kyujin (1868–1933), a painter and calligrapher accomplished in many different styles and a cofounder of the Calligraphy Association.

Sit in the pavilion and a cold wind blows up, as if from the polar regions, and my eyes seem to reach out endlessly into the distance. To the far right floats the dim shape of the Outer Diamond Mountains, and to the northeast an infinite country of water. To the east of the East Sea there is little sense of the east.

It is a fine background for arousing a sense of the military spirit of these rocky cliffs, which stand to attention, awesomely still despite all the waves of the East Sea that seem to drive up against this one spot. As scenery it is perhaps too dreadful to enjoy. Could these really be called birds, these seagulls that seem to swoop joyfully in and out of these rocks in pairs? I return on the six o'clock bus.

Record of a Journey to Manchuria

An Enormous Space

I took a night train to Pongch'ŏn, after spending the day in Pyongyang at the instigation of friends I had met on the train.*

It was my first trip north of Pyongyang in more than twenty years, and the first time in my life that I had gone north of Andong Province. Anju, Chŏngju, Sŏnch'ŏn, Ŭiju . . . these are all places in my memory that I would like to see again, places that I had passed through on foot after my money had run out in Andong Province

---

* Pongch'ŏn was the first city of Manchukuo, also known as Fengtian in Chinese, Hōten in Japanese, and Mukden in English. This reflects Manchuria's multilingual residents of the time. Before and after Manchukuo, it was and is now once more known as Shenyang. Yi uses Chinese characters to write place names in this travelogue, with the exception of the immigrants' village, for which he gives the *han'gŭl* inscription of the Chinese reading of the characters. This translation uses the Korean pronunciation of all Manchu place names written in Chinese characters.

as a boy. But, as it was the night train, I had no option other than to close the curtain and try to get some sleep.

The lower bunk in a third-class cabin . . . it was good not having to perform the acrobatic trick of climbing up and down to the top bunk, but with someone less than three feet from my face, and then yet someone else lying above that person, the atmosphere was heavy and claustrophobic, as if I was at the bottom holding them all up. I had laid down still wearing my jacket with all its pockets full of stuff, so it was uncomfortable to turn over even. I could try to remove the jacket, but there was no obvious place to hang it, let alone somewhere it might lay folded up. I did try to sit up in an effort to straighten my clothes out at least, but I hit my head on the bunk above me. I tried sitting, too, with my neck bent like a crane, but lying down turned out to be more comfortable after all. A space as large as my body should suffice lying down, but in truth I could not manage to shed all worldly desire like a bag on a shelf. I thought of that philosopher who once lived in a barrel. But it appears that some training is necessary to be able to gather one's thoughts in a third-class berth.

The continent . . . is a landscape for which I have long yearned. When I was in Tokyo, there was once an exhibition of new Russian art. A landscape painting that I saw there, titled "Rainbow," is still freshly imprinted on my mind today. It showed an endless horizon stretching out in the clearest of colors after rainfall, fields scattered here and there with no roads in sight, and a rainbow with just two roots sunk in a field like an arched gate, reaching out over the widest of spaces. I have from time to time seen landscape paintings in other exhibitions since then, but never such an enormous space as in that one.

An enormous space . . . that is what impresses itself upon us in Russian novels. When China pressed down upon our Eastern State over those several centuries in the past, that must also have been through the machination of its enormous space.

My train was cutting through the night, racing toward that continent, that space.

At first, the idea of "going there," whether that meant to the people or to nature or whatever, seemed to have excited me, for even
after midnight I could not sleep. Finally, when the train reached
Andong Province and the customs officials jumped on, the car-
riages grew noisy. Everyone got up, and all the luggage was pulled
out. I opened up my bag for inspection too. The train stood still
for thirty minutes and, as if loudspeakers maketh the border, announcements were constantly repeated from beginning to end for
the entire duration of the stop.

With the train departed once more, all the passengers laid down
again. "They will sleep through these places!" I suddenly realized and
thought of Sŏng Sammun.* Back when Sejong was creating these
letters with which I now write, he ordered Sammun to go to Huang
Zan, a scholar at the Ming Royal Academy, and ask about phono-
logical structure. It is said that Sammun went to and from Huang's
place of exile on the Liaodong Peninsula a total of thirteen times.

Back then he would have traveled by horse at best. Each day he
would have covered sixty or seventy *li*. When I think of it now, lying
down as we travel a thousand *li* on the night train, it seems like a
legend from a very long time ago! He did not even make one or two
return journeys, but thirteen all together. Sŏng Sammun's sense of
service was amazing, and I can only bow before Sejong's resolute
statesmanship.

The train seems to be racing along in a straight line without
a single curve. On this enormous earth, through this enormous
space and the night that covers it, this train is like a tiny mudfish,
crawling along the ocean bed.

---

* Sŏng Sammun (1418–1456) was one of the scholars who aided King Sejong
  (r. 1418–1450) during the creation of the *han'gŭl* alphabet.

Earth, Earth

In a wink I was asleep, and when I awoke the window across from me was dimly lit. Dawn must have broken! I lifted the curtain at my head without rising from my bunk. White specks passed by in the distance, but this was the westward side and it was still more night than day. When I looked at my watch, five o'clock had long passed. Even here the sun seemed to rise somewhat later than in Seoul. I got up and washed before going to the dining car with its wide windows. Houses passed by in a hazy mist. Their silhouette was different from that of the farmhouses in Korea. There were only straight lines. It was as if one long building had been cut into pieces: a windowless wall rose up with the roof cut off and no eaves to either the left or the right. These were the kind of houses that painters in the Oriental style usually paint in Korea too.

In a continuous stretch of countless straight lines, long-furrowed fields opened up and folded in layers, like the ribs of a fan. There was nothing to block either the back of the villages or the edges of the fields. There was, of course, not a single mountain or hill in sight. A field would pass by, and then another one in succession, and just when the eye grew bored a group of five or six poplars would appear, followed by a drab farming village that looked as if it had been cut out with a knife. Gradually, people in indigo clothing could be seen one by one on the roads, and then there were signs I could read from inside the carriage—here too they read "Jintan Pharmaceuticals," "Ajinomoto," and the like. The scenery was the same for miles around. A layer of thin ice covered the ditches, while white frost lay over the rice stalks in the fields. Wherever I looked in the distant mist, the line between earth and sky was murky. Not a single wall, but earth and more earth, the dark color of ground acorns, and the wide, flat ridges of fields, which looked as if a horse had galloped along trailing a line behind it. Beyond that field lie more of those same ridges, a world of furrowed fields that does not disappear no matter how far ahead our express train races. Inside the carriage, I did not even realize I had unfastened my jacket button and taken a long gulp of breath at this field of vision, which was as vast as might be seen from the peak of some great mountain. Before my eyes passes an image of the red faces, their veins protruding, that first lay this railroad on an ocean of earth, with no target other than the drifting clouds in the sky, and that still clutched to their hammers as they embarked on the first test journey. All stages allow glory to their main players alone.

Of those who sit at this window and gaze out upon the unbounded earth, it must be our immigrants who are most moved by its essential nature as earth—yes, they who have left behind a homeland because it would not offer them any earth. At first, they must have been surprised, exclaiming, "Ah, there's so much land!"

Then, when they saw those people in blue clothes who stood at the head of each field with tools in their hands and stared joylessly at the passing train, our immigrants must have thought, "But, wait, all these fields have owners, don't they?"

The dreams in their tired heads, born of an arid life, must have made them dizzy.

After we had traveled for a while, past some station ending in the character *tun*, meaning "camp," a large stop appeared by the name of Sogadun.* Here we stopped for more than four minutes. The station workers and policemen all wore yellowish uniforms. Once we had left Sogadun, the conductor appeared and announced that we would soon arrive at Pongch'ŏn. That was the final stop for this train, and I thought that, having come this far, I should get some idea of the place during the few hours I would have to spend here.

I disembarked the train in the early morning, just before eight o'clock. The low morning sun pierced the dark shadows of the

---

* *Sujiatun* in Chinese.

unfamiliar buildings and deserted streets of this foreign city and dazzled my eyes. I turned back to the waiting room at the station.

A Sense of Kin

No sooner had I entered the station than a salty smell, like an ocean breeze, penetrated my nostrils. It was the body odor emanating from the clothes of a people for whom water is truly precious. The posters and articles in the store were exactly the same as those at Kyŏngsŏng Station.* I bought a *Guide to Pongch'ŏn* and went into the third-class waiting room. People in white clothes were dotted here and there among the crowd that packed the room to capacity. The people covered in what seemed to be Pongch'ŏn dirt were probably rickshaw drivers, whereas those with bloodshot eyes blinking listlessly, or those snoring away despite being curled up on their bundles in any spot just large enough for crouching, appeared to be the so-called free immigrants from our homeland. They had arrived by train either last night or this morning and were waiting to transfer. A young man wore a winter cap but no coat, an old lady sat next to a grandson with disheveled hair and mumbled away as she ate fried beans, and at their side were bundles wrapped in faded indigo or thin, worn quilts dangling pieces of gourd, both large and small, like hotel address labels. I went up to the old lady and asked her where she was heading. She continued to crunch on the beans as she pulled a crumpled brown envelope from her trouser top and showed it to me. On it was written an address of somewhere near the Moran River. Apparently her youngest son had moved there three years earlier and had not starved, and so he had asked her to come stay with him and avoid hunger for her remaining days. She

---

* Kyŏngsŏng is the Korean pronunciation of *Keijō*, the Japanese name for Seoul during the colonial period.

had left a village called Suinch'ŏn in P'yŏngan Province together with one of her eldest son's children.

I went to the second-class waiting room where there was also not a single free seat. Next I tried the washroom, where I found a woman in Korean dress had taken off her bright red cotton top and was washing her neck, even though it was not a ladies-only facility. At second glance, I realized there were several Korean women beside her: a swarthy woman who looked to have left thirty way behind, a young girl with fluffy down who could not have been more than sixteen or seventeen, and three more women of around twenty-two or three, including the one washing her neck. They were brassy, healthy-looking women, although not of particularly fair complexion. They had pulled out red and blue bottles from which cheap perfume wafted around and were busying themselves with their toilet. I approached the woman who finished applying her makeup first.

"Excuse me, but this is my first time here. May I ask where you are all heading?"

"What?"

She was surprised, and then all of their eyes, which had been fixed upon me, turned toward an older gentleman off to one side who had looked as if he had nothing to do with them. This yellow-bearded gentleman flashed a pair of small, sharp eyes and stroked a gold watch chain with one hand as he walked toward me.

"Excuse me, but will the train to Shingyŏng arrive soon?"*

"You don't look like the kind of man who would have to ask the time of a train . . . "

His eyes grew even sharper. I feigned innocence, saying, "It is precisely because I don't know that I'm asking. Aren't you going to Shingyŏng?"

"We're headed north."

---

* *Xinjing* in Chinese.

He looked me up and down with a glance and then headed off to the store where he bought enough five *chŏn* packs of *Miruku* to give one each to the women. They gulped them down as if they were famished. Each flashed a golden tooth and called the old man "father." No doubt he was the boss of some inn or pavilion somewhere like Beijing or Tientsin. I could not help but feel a new sense of kinship with the fishy-smelling flesh of these young girls, who painted their eyebrows as they chewed on *Miruku* and seemed so carefree and happy despite being dragged off to a dangerous foreign country.

The Pongch'ŏn Museum

Following my *Guide to Pongch'ŏn,* I took a taxi to the Yamato Hotel. This elegant four-story inn, said to be of the "American renaissance" style, soared to one side of a large square that had a war memorial celebrating victory at its center. A chalk palace with many open corridors, it seemed more suited to the luscious greenery of southern countries than here in the north. I entrusted my bag and coat to the clerk, and went straight to the dining room. Blue-eyed ladies and gentlemen sat in corners drinking fragrant coffee and eating colorful fruit. I too took breakfast according to the fresh morning menu and then visited the travel bureau to order my ticket for the Asea Special Express train to Shingyŏng. Only then did I go out into the streets. As if out of nowhere, two rickshaws came running up at the same time. They were far lower than rickshaws in Korea and looked luxurious with small lanterns hanging on both sides and colorful tassels dangling down by the seat. I sat in the cleaner-looking of the two and gave the order,

"*Hakubutsukan!*"

The driver flashed his yellow teeth, but clearly did not understand. Even when I took out my map and showed him where the museum was, he did not seem to recognize the city, but he ran off with me in tow anyway so as not to lose a customer. We made our way for a while with me shouting at him to stop and taking out my map every time I saw someone who looked as if they might be able to read. They would invariably make a noise among themselves for a while and finally not be able to help the driver find the museum. For his part, the driver kept on running forward. No doubt he calculated that he would earn more running along than resting, no matter whether his customer reached his destination or not. In the end, I had to fight my way off this blindly running rickshaw and switch to a taxi.

The three-story chalk pavilion at the intersection of Third and Tenth Streets was once the private residence of Tang Yulin of the former northeast military faction. Its important collections include bronzeware from the Zhou-Han period, pottery from the golden ages of Liao and Song, and calligraphy since the Song and Yuan dynasties. Its woven silk and embroidery are all noteworthy examples of the crafts of dyeing and weaving. I unexpectedly discovered some colored pottery engraved in free brush style and a woodblock print by the Frenchman Caussin of an original picture by the world-famous G. B. Castiglione.* Although the Oriental paintings were mostly landscapes, there were many interesting paintings on fans. Altogether more than thirty-five hundred works easily give the impression of the vitality, leisure, delicacy, and maturity of the continental peoples, but there was nothing that could appeal to a more sensitive nature in the manner of the sentimentality and humor of the Koryŏ and Yi dynasties. Moreover, in terms of both quality and quantity, it is a rather weak museum in that it does not give a sense of the importance of Pongch'ŏn as the home of the great Qing Empire that ruled the Han people. I regret that I came

---

* Giuseppe Castiglione (1688–1766) was an Italian painter and Jesuit who went to China as a missionary in 1715 and lived out the rest of his life there. He was a favorite of the Emperor Qianlong, who appreciated his painting and also had Castiglione design several palaces.

to Manchuria but did not get to see the Taeryŏn Museum, said to be the best museum in the East.*

Next I took a coach to the Hall of Common Good. As the Hall of Common Good is an institution that has deep relations with poor people, the coach driver understood me easily.

The Hall of Common Good

The Hall of Common Good is a large charitable institution that takes in more than seven hundred unfortunate souls, including orphans, beggars, and paupers, as well as *kisaeng* and barmaids, prostitutes and illegitimate children. It was founded more than thirty years ago as the operation of an individual named Zuo Baogui and has become one of Pongch'ŏn's most well-known sites, deserving special mention for its facilities and the morality it displays, both of which are of a kind rarely found in orphanages or old people's homes.

From the office, where a large plaque reads "Never tire of doing good," countless buildings in both the Western and Chinese single-story style lead back to the right and the left. There is a hospital, carpenter's workshop, printing shop, textile factory, and even a kindergarten and school, but the places that leave the deepest impression are the maternity wing, the rehabilitation hall, and the life-saving gate. Naturally the hall takes in old people who are no longer capable of supporting themselves, but it also accepts all kinds of prostitutes, including women forced into prostitution and bar girls who have fled abusive employers. It offers such women proper guidance and even protects women who have been beaten by their husbands. In the case of such women, their husbands usually come asking for reconciliation within three months; for those women with no one to take them away, whether prostitutes,

---

* *Taeryŏn* is *Dairen* in Japanese and *Dalian* in Chinese.

virgins, or wives, the hall finds stable marriage partners. Because these women tend to be good at running households, requests for a bride are received from all sorts of men, from bachelors to widowers. An even stranger sight is the "life-saving" gate at the maternity wing, where in order to prevent the killing of illegitimate babies any woman who asks for help with childbirth is welcome, even if she is clearly not poor. No one asks the woman's name, address, or circumstances of pregnancy. Once her child has been born, she may leave it at the hall, while she covers up her traces and moves on with her life. The actual gate is tall and located in a back alley. A basket, which is just large enough to hold a young child, is placed in a hole inside the gate; if a child is placed in the basket it presses down and rings a bell. Anyone who is struggling to raise a child can leave it in this basket and walk away without going through any formal process or even showing her face. This is a holy institution: it simply helps the unfortunate, irrespective of their sins.

When I reemerged it was past one in the afternoon, or thirteen o'clock, as they say here. I took a coach into town and passed once through the business district, with its dust and smattering of gold and red signs. Back at the hotel I picked up my bag and hurried off to the station without even time to eat lunch.

The dark-green bulletlike streamlined form of the Asea Special Express runs between Taeryŏn and Habi and is known as the fastest train in the whole of the East.* It left Pongch'ŏn with no time to rest and picked up speed immediately, running lightly at a constant speed with almost no vibration. The sensation is a bit like having one's head shaved with one of those new shaving machines. Outside the window there is nothing but flat plains. I thought of my friends who like mountain climbing and wondered what would happen if they came to live somewhere like this. It was funny to think that, depending on the person, even a flat plain could be hell.

---

* *Habi* refers to *Haerbin* and is better known as Harbin in English.

I ate lunch in the dining car, where all the waitresses were Russian. One was white, very pale, and had a square forehead, which made her look like Sonya in the film "Crime and Punishment." White Russian daughters with no nationality, poor young girls who spend their lives looking out onto the monotonous plains without even a homeland to embrace with their homesickness . . . the cup of coffee served by them emitted a whiff of romance that was almost as strong as alcohol. While I sipped repeatedly on that coffee, I worried about becoming a lonely shadow on the endless plain where I was to visit an immigrant village the following day.

Shingyŏng

We arrived in Shingyŏng after six in the evening. A cold wind clipped my ears as I came out the station; streets radiated out from the square and seemed to disappear into the dusky night. The buildings, both old and new, were all dark as if empty. I pulled up my coat collar and waited a while for a small taxi. I asked to be taken to the *Mansŏn ilbo* newspaper building on Yŏngch'ang Street. We drove down the largest street in front of us; it was asphalted and the hills were laid with stones that rippled out in waves like pieces of bean curd. The town was not all flat, but had high and low areas that reminded me of Tokyo. Every two or three large buildings or so we would pass a boarded fence with a sign saying this company or that store was under construction.

As there were few pedestrians on the street, the cars could drive however they liked. After about fifteen minutes, we stopped in front of a building with a red flag.

My friends Hoengbo, Yŏsu, and T'aeu were still at work and greeted me joyfully.* I felt as if I had come to the ends of the

---

* Hoengbo is the novelist Yŏm Sangsŏp (1897–1963), Yŏsu the poet Pak P'aryang (1905–?), and T'aeu refers to Yi T'aeu, an editor at the *Mansŏn ilbo*

earth, and these familiar friends who were working and living here seemed like different people entirely as they sat at their desks. We immediately set off for Yŏsu's house, where we ate a freshly prepared dinner in front of the cozy pechka fireplace while indulging in tales of Shingyŏng and of the immigrant villages and lamenting our own situations.* Then, with T'aeu in the lead, we went outside to see Shingyŏng at night.

The sun had long set, but the far western horizon of the sky still glowed azure. Bright stars shone and a soft wind blew; all I could hear was the jangling of coach bells, the clip-clopping of hooves, and the cracking of whips passing by from near and far. All the lights in the houses were dim, as if they were under attack, and the strong outer gates were shut already in the early evening. We took a coach and gazed up at the flickering stars in the sky as we headed toward the masses of neon signs in town. First we went to a dance hall called Monte Carlo where a whole room full of men and women gently swayed to a doleful waltz, like duckweed on the surface of a pond. T'aeu was the only one of us to jump into their midst, while Yŏsu sat drinking tea with me; even if he were to live in Shingyŏng ten more years he would never manage to learn to dance, he said. Next we took another coach for some ten *li* to find an inn run by Manchus, but they were all full. We had no choice but to find some other inn and by eleven o'clock were out on the street again. We visited one of the brothels here known as *kaip'anzi*. They are shaped like inns from the outside, but inside a hall opens out like a courtyard, surrounded on all sides by three or four floors of guest rooms connected by corridors and rails. We were led up to a room on the second floor that was furnished with a teakettle on a table, some wooden stools, a wide bed, a mirror and a dressing table. After Yŏsu had undertaken some negotiations, a great clamor began, as sudden as if a light had been turned on, and some dozen Manchu

---

* Pechka is an all-in-one stove, oven, and fireplace used in Russia.

girls came rushing into our room from all directions. Three that we pointed out remained behind as the others all left again. Each hour spent eating watermelon seeds and talking costs one *wŏn*, but after midnight the nature of the business takes a sudden turn and they become prostitutes. Yŏsu and T'aeu were happily laughing and chatting, but for me, who knew only the one word of Manchu *manmandi*,* it was like cows and chickens. Frustrated, we did not even stay a full hour, but came out and passed by a street where many white Russians live. Their drinking establishments, known as cabarets, have their own music bands and dancers, although any guest can go there to enjoy dancing in the exotic atmosphere. At any moment the crowds include a mixture of five races—Russians, Manchurians, Germans, Greeks, and then us.

In front of every ten or so of the closed businesses that we passed on our way back a black shadow was either sitting or standing. These guards had been posted to deter robbers and would have to stand or sit throughout the long night even in a cold of minus forty degrees. For each evening of work, they earn one *wŏn* and a few *chŏn*. Apparently only white Russians do this work. What a depressing street and nightlife!

Jiangjiawopu

When I woke up the next day I went to Yŏsu and asked him to introduce me to several people who knew about the situation in the immigrant villages.

I learned that the place with the longest history was also the place that had seen the biggest problems, and that was the area of Manbosan where the first huge water ditch built with Korean hands flowed through the wasteland. Of the several villages in Manbosan

---

* A Chinese phrase meaning "slowly."

the most convenient to reach from Shingyŏng was a place called Jiangjiawopu. But, when I asked, even traveling there turned out to be far from easy. From Shingyŏng one had to take a train going to Paeksŏngja,* get off at the second stop, and walk at least thirty Korean *li* before immigrant houses would begin to appear. There were only two trains a day—in the morning and evening—and I had already missed the morning train. Then there was the problem of the thirty *li*. Not only was it an empty plain without many houses, but I would not be able to ask the way, as I knew no Manchu. I tried, without success, to negotiate for a coach and then asked about small taxis, to no avail either. Having come this far, I wanted to visit a village where new immigrants were digging their hoes into virgin ground, but to see such a village it seemed I would have to go to Kando Province or somewhere where group settlement was underway. Because that was happening under the aegis of either the Mansen Colonization Company or state policy, it would be hard to visit without some kind of position, and, in any event, this would mean going to such places as Ando Province. To reach these would involve getting off at a station called Myŏngwŏlgu,† from where the nearest settlement was some fifty or sixty *li* and the next some one or two hundred *li* into the heartland. Apparently, in such places the situation is so precarious that the protection of a policeman or guard is necessary, even if all one wants to do is chop down a tree. Traveling there alone would involve arming myself as a prerequisite, and even then, without some kind of firm resolution, I might not return. Just as I had given up on reaching those new settlements and decided to visit somewhere like Jiangjiawopu in Manbosan, the news came that a group of Koreans from there were at this moment in Shingyŏng and would be

---

* *Baichengzi* in Chinese.

† *Mingyuegou* in Chinese.

returning on the train the following morning. I spent a relaxed day in Shingyŏng before heading out the next day for the train. Both Yŏsu and T'aeu came along and helped me meet up with a young Korean boy wearing Manchu clothes. He introduced us to two people wearing Korean-style winter coats and a middle-aged couple who were so-called free immigrants. The wife was sitting with a young baby on her back and a young girl held close to her, while the husband wore no outer coat but carried a pack the size of a mountain and dangling gourds. He looked around nervously, having nowhere to rest his load. The carriage reeked of a smell that seemed to come from the blue clothes and dirty copper coins. We were supposed to depart, but it was *manmandi* . . . more like a succession of postponements than an attempt to embark on a journey.

My traveling companions had come to Shingyŏng to sell hemp cloth and pigs. Usually they sell their grain in one lot in the autumn to other Koreans who own rice-processing businesses, but if they need some extra money and have rice left over, they sometimes sell it in smaller amounts. In town they buy cloth, socks, ointment, soap, matches, chinaware, thread, needles, pots, seeds, and writing paper. One had even bought a gramophone record. It was something called the "New Tobacco Song." Protruding from one bundle was a piece of board used to coil cloth that must have come from a linen shop. Here there are two precious commodities: stone and wood. It is impossible to buy stone, and so hardly any houses are built on foundation stones. Instead they use even a piece of board the size of a nameplate that can be bought in Shingyŏng.

"The leaves must be coming out in Korea around now?"

"Have the azaleas bloomed on the sunny slopes?"

Their eyes misted over as they asked me questions, recalling the homeland that they had left behind some five, six, or even ten years before. The mother swiveled the baby on her back around to her breast. The eyes, which had been startled with all the noise going on around her, now lit up that gaunt face with a faint smile as she looked down at her child. Her husband stood still at her side with nowhere to sit.

Gourd Dippers

Fifty minutes later we got off at a station called Sohamnyung.* An armed guard stood at the station, inspecting every single bundle and letting people pass one by one. The station buildings were made from brick and the lower half of their doors covered in steel so that, if necessary, the entire station could become a fortress and respond to attack. Outside the station there were two railway office buildings, a hut run by natives that served as a bar, and then the plain. It was hard to tell if there was a road at all.

"Anyone who needs water should drink it here before we head off."

We went into the bar, from which some people seemed to emerge having drunk more than water. Apparently there would not be much chance of finding something along the way. Some people carried cloth bundles under their arms and on their backs. The mother carried her child on her back, while her young daughter clung tightly to her mother's skirt and dragged her large rubber shoes noisily, and the head of the family adjusted his shoulder strap so as to carry all of their belongings on his back. I walked behind them all, watching the gourd dippers dangling from his bundle.

How Koreans like their gourd dippers! They use them to scoop fresh water, rinse rice, beat out tunes, and even feed a new mother her first meal.

Wherever Koreans go, they dream of living beneath a roof entangled with gourd vines; the tale of the brothers Hŭngbu and Nol-

---

*   *Xiaohelong* in Chinese.

bu breaking the gourd in half must be the eternal truth, morality, and joy of these simple people.* In this northern country, where the frost attacks before the gourd has time to ripen, those pieces of gourd brought from the homeland are ancestral utensils, the only album to invoke memories of the old home.

No matter how far we walk, the scenery never changes. One by one native houses appear, with their mud walls and mud roofs, but unfortunately they never disappear again from sight. We meet just one person driving a herd of some dozens of pigs, and a family in a horse-drawn cart who seem to be going to Shingyŏng, but otherwise we do not even see crows or other birds.

"Where did you come from?"

"We're from Kijang," replied the owner of the gourd-laden bundle. According to him, Kijang is somewhere near Tongnae in South Kyŏngsang Province. Some of his neighbors had moved here first and urged him to come too, saying there was plenty of farmland.

Once we had walked some fifteen *li* to the northwest, a yellow stream of unknown depth flowed by, dragging pieces of ice. They told me that the immigrants had built a dam upstream, where the land is somewhat higher, and use this stream to irrigate their rice paddies. We sat down to rest for a while in the middle of the road, because there was not a single rock anywhere on which we might sit. Then we walked a further fifteen *li* before

---

* The tale of Hŭngbu and Nolbu tells the story of two brothers: Hŭngbu is rich but mean, whereas Nolbu is poor and honest. One day Nolbu cures an injured swallow who later returns with a seed. The seed produces a rich crop of gourds, which when split reveal many treasures. Hearing this, Hŭngbu deliberately injures a swallow and then cures it. This swallow also returns with a seed, but when the gourds from this plant are cracked open, monsters emerge and destroy Hŭngbu's house. Nolbu takes Hŭngbu and his family in, and they both live happy and honest lives ever after.

rice paddies began to appear. In the paddies, the rice plants had been planted firm and deep, but the rows were not planted evenly and the dykes were crooked too, as if made by children. For the first time in a while, I saw white washing spread out on a fence. Then yellow thatched roofs and stacks of straw appeared on the far horizon. It looked as if we would have to walk a long way to reach them. A ditch appeared. This was the ditch of the infamous Manbosan incident.*

It was a large water ditch some twelve to thirteen feet wide at the bottom, twenty-one to twenty-two feet wide at the top, and more than twenty *li* in length. Many local coolies had also helped, but it was mostly the sweat and blood of our own immigrants that had brought this large-scale project to completion.

By the side of the dry ditch a girl in Korean clothes, looking some ten years old, carried a baby on her back and stood still watching us. A hill of golden turf or a riverbank of golden sand must seem like the stuff of fantasy to her.

The Village with a Full Stomach

We passed the village by the ditch but still had to walk a while before we reached the larger village of Jiangjiawopu, which has a school. The building with a red tin roof was the school. The village was even dirtier than the empty plain. Here and there were bogs so that we had to choose our steps carefully, and pigs passed by in herds. Viewed close up, the houses were buried behind kaoliang stalk

---

* The Manbosan incident of 1931 involved a dispute between Chinese and Korean settlers over a water ditch the Koreans had built on Chinese land. The incident was misreported in a sensationalist fashion in the Korean and Japanese press, provoking many cases of violence against Chinese residents and property all over Korea, as a result of which many Chinese died.

fences. There were stacks of bound kaoliang stalks and straw, and thus dried grass everywhere. It looked as if the whole village would burn down if just one cigarette were dropped. Children appeared from behind this and that fence, dogs ran out, and chickens had to be chased away. Each of my companions invited me to his house for lunch. I went into the home of Mr. Pak, who wore Chinese clothes.

Mr. Pak's house was also surrounded by a kaoliang stalk fence over which the wind howled. There was a mountain of rice straw and kaoliang stalks in the yard. They burn grasses throughout the year here because there is no firewood. We walked through a door at the center of the straight-lined house and into a kitchen with an earthen floor. There were rooms to both sides with earthen floors as well, a high Chinese-style heated floor known as a k'ang, and an empty space just large enough for removing shoes. Reed mats covered the k'ang.

I looked out the windows from where I sat on the mats. To the south there was a window large enough to have sliding doors fitted horizontally; the walls had been papered with the *Mansŏn ilbo* newspaper and a map of Manchuria hung. On the northern side they had spread reed mats, which were not large enough and so they had also used piles of grass. Looking out through the glass fitted into the window, I could see a thatched hut about the height of a man, three armfuls round and tied several times with kaoliang stalks. Inside there were no husks, as one might expect, but the rice that they would eat, as they did not have a separate store-room. When I asked whether they had no problems with mice eating their rice, the reply was "well, how much could they possibly eat?" Chickens and pigs also poke around from time to time. I was happy to hear that they were so generous with their grain, as it did not seem that feeding a guest would be too much trouble for them. I was hungry. My legs ached. Not a single sound could be heard. Only the sky showed through the window glass; open the window and all there would be was the dazzling white space across which we had just panted, as though swimming. The enormity of the monotony stifled me. All energy to ask questions or even to think evaporated in an instant. In such an environment all I wanted was to let my mouth drop open like an idiot and lie down.

My spirits revived somewhat at the sight of the lunch table. There was plain boiled rice, which was so yellow it looked like brown rice. The soup was made from dried radish leaves, and somehow we each had a shrimp too. There was pickled cabbage, in which the pepper seeds were more radiant than the peppers themselves, and then whole peppers placed on a small brass dish. It looked as if they had first dried any peppers that had grown old and gray or had frozen black and then steamed them in a rice pot. I waited for the man to begin eating so that I could see how to eat them; he just dipped them in soy sauce. I tried one, all the time breathing heavily. Even with just these three side dishes, which were almost in their original form as raw ingredients, the taste was the sweetest I have experienced since my intestinal problems of the year before last. I ate all four heaped bowls of rice that they offered me.

"Now we just fill our stomachs with anything . . . " With these words Mr. Pak urged me to eat more rice. I repressed my urge to lie down, though I kept yawning with drowsiness, and began to ask him about this and that.

Local Legends

"What kind of things do you farm?"

"Rice, millet, kaoliang, buckwheat, soybeans, corn, and pota-toes . . . usually these, and, of course, vegetables too."

"Do people who come to live here generally share the same standard of living?"

"I can't say that we are all the same. It's already been several years, hasn't it, since the Manbosan incident erupted in Jiangjia-wopu? This is probably the most established of all the immigrant villages. When inspection parties come, they are usually brought to this village."

"Do you all own the land in this village?"

"There are hardly any of us who own our land. Because we all rent from Manchurians, this is really tenant farming. The first people who came here to Manbosan got together to collect enough money to rent some wasteland."

"Oh, could you explain exactly how that worked?"

"We paid a percentage to someone local and rented five hundred *sang* of land (one *sang* is the equivalent of two thousand *p'yŏng*) from a rich Manchurian in Changch'un. I've forgotten now how that contract worked."

"I see."

"But the native Manchurians in this area all protested vigorously."

"Why?"

"They were angry because they said that if Koreans came here and planted rice paddies their own fields would be ruined."

"Why would their fields be ruined?"

"You must have noticed on the way here that all these plains are just like laminated floors? That's why the water from the paddies has nowhere to drain away. It just spreads out in all directions as it likes, and so if there are fields to the side they are in truth ruined."

"Well, couldn't those people also change their fields to paddies?"

"They have no notion how to follow. Some say that if they eat rice then they need side dishes as well, and then that they get stomachaches. Even if they do farm rice they have no idea how to sell it . . . So they think that it's safest just to grow what they will eat in their own fields."

"How did the opposition movement come about?"

"Well, it was those same people who rushed about when they heard we were going to dig a big water ditch more than twenty feet wide. Some several hundred people ran to the government office. They said they would lose their living because of us Koreans, and, even though the office had given us permission to reclaim land, it irresponsibly denied all knowledge of this. The people stopped selling food to Koreans and wouldn't let us use their wells. When I think about that time . . . well, finally it became a matter of life and death, and we had no option but to fight back. We had used all the food and money that we had brought with us on renting the land and building the ditch, which was almost finished. Where could we go when they told us to leave? We had no travel money, and if we moved we would need money to set up farming, wouldn't we? Even if they paid us compensation, think of the blood and sweat we had expended on a ditch of twenty *li* . . . still they kept on telling us to move. The natives kept on filling in the ditch we had dug in places. Then we would run and threaten to kill them and dig it out again. It may sound funny, but this was a battle over life and death. We would even dig through the night. Later on the natives went back to the government office and raised a commotion, so that finally the Chinese army came out and started firing their guns. Bullets were flying over our heads, but we just kept on shoveling the dirt out of the ditch; after all, what difference did it make whether we died one way or another?"

He rubbed his dry forehead several times, as if that scene were still fresh before his eyes.

If the Mountain Is Not High, the Water Won't Run Clear

Mr. Pak said that no one was actually hit by a bullet back then. Maybe it was because they were threatened from afar and the bullets shot past them through the air. Several youths were captured and locked up for some days before being released, but that was all. He regretted greatly that the bloodshed had occurred in Korea.

Aside from the army attack, if natives had really enjoyed taking lives, they could easily have made the Koreans victims of their clubs.

He took me on a tour of the village and the school. There were no more than twenty houses in all, and they were spread out without a center. They were the same shape as Mr. Pak's home, sitting inside a kaoliang stalk fence as if folding their arms and basking in the sun. Since the sowing happens late, and the harvest early, the slack time in the farming schedule here is at least twice as long as in Korea. Brewing is unregulated, and once the alcohol is ready neighbors enjoy inviting each other to drink. The pleasure of individuals lies in dreams of winning the lottery. The tickets for the ten-thousand *wŏn* lottery can be bought from Manchukuo for one *wŏn* each. Anyone who lives here can buy them, and each month one person will be a winner, which means that you spend one *wŏn* and win ten thousand. Among the Koreans here, an old woman who sold oil in Shingyŏng and a young lad who worked as a clerk at some company had both won.

"If we could win the lottery, we would go back and live in our homeland again! Otherwise we have to live like this day by day and be buried at the head of a Manchu's field!"

This was the source of their hope as well as their sadness.

The school was built by stacking up earthen bricks known as *t'ukoe*, laying a tin roof on top, and inserting glass windows. The floor was made of earth and not wood. He told me that up to two hundred children from the villages within ten or twenty *li* gather here. It was holiday time, so only seven or eight children from this village were kicking around a worn-out football. This place had been established and run by the immigrant villages at first, but now Manchukuo had taken the schools over and was running it according to their policies. It would not be long before the textbooks and teachers changed. In fact, because the whole area of Manbosan lay adjacent to the capital and was not a Korean immigrant zone, one could never know when it might be subject to reorganization like the border region.

At three in the afternoon I set out alone from Jiangjiawopu to catch the seven o'clock train to Sohamnyung.

When I thought about how, within a day or two, I would enter my homeland of embroidered rivers and mountains, which had been given the name Koryŏ because of its high mountains and clear waters, I had not the heart to look back at those people remaining on this vast plain.

I walked with my head down. When I reached the earlier village by the water ditch I found three boys of eight or nine years old. They wore glasses fashioned from kaoliang stalks, pretended to smoke the kaoliang stalks they had rolled up like tobacco, and sang this song:

Yukuri, ch'ŏnch'ŏnhi, manmandi
*Tabakko handae ch'ŏuwenba**

I later found out that *ch'ŏuwenba* was a Manchu word meaning "let's smoke tobacco."

An hour later, the thatched roofs and fences covered in white washing had all disappeared. Not a single bird flew through the air. There was only the sound of my footsteps plodding along like those of a young child. Several times I stood still and strained my ears. Not a sound came from anywhere.

The eternity was even more desolate than the ocean.

---

*   The song suggests the role of Manchuria at the center of the Greater East Asia Co-Prosperity Sphere: the first line repeats the word for "slowly" in Japanese, Korean, and then Chinese, whereas the second line takes the same three languages to make the sentence "Let's smoke a cigarette."

Weatherhead Books on Asia

WEATHERHEAD EAST ASIAN INSTITUTE, COLUMBIA UNIVERSITY

Literature   **DAVID DER-WEI WANG, EDITOR**

Ye Zhaoyan, *Nanjing 1937: A Love Story*, translated by Michael Berry (2003)

Oda Makato, *The Breaking Jewel*, translated by Donald Keene (2003)

Han Shaogong, *A Dictionary of Maqiao*, translated by Julia Lovell (2003)

Takahashi Takako, *Lonely Woman*, translated by Maryellen Toman Mori (2004)

Chen Ran, *A Private Life*, translated by John Howard-Gibbon (2004)

Eileen Chang, *Written on Water*, translated by Andrew F. Jones (2004)

Writing Women in Modern China: The Revolutionary Years, 1936-1976, edited by
    Amy D. Dooling (2005)

Han Bangqing, *The Sing-song Girls of Shanghai*, first translated by Eileen Chang,
    revised and edited by Eva Hung (2005)

Loud Sparrows: Contemporary Chinese Short-Shorts, translated and edited by Aili Mu,
    Julie Chiu, Howard Goldblatt (2006)

Hiratsuka Raichō, *In the Beginning, Woman Was the Sun*, translated by Teruko Craig
    (2006)

Zhu Wen, *I Love Dollars and Other Stories of China*, translated by Julia Lovell (2007)

Kim Sowŏl, *Azaleas: A Book of Poems*, translated by David McCann (2007)

Wang Anyi, *The Song of Everlasting Sorrow: A Novel of Shanghai*, translated by
    Michael Berry with Susan Chan Egan (2008)

Ch'oe Yun, *There a Petal Silently Falls: Three Stories by Ch'oe Yun*, translated by
    Bruce and Ju-Chan Fulton (2008)

Inoue Yasushi, *The Blue Wolf: A Novel of the Life of Chinggis Khan*, translated by
    Joshua A. Fogel (2009)

Anonymous, *Courtesans and Opium: Romantic Illusions of the Fool of Yangzhou*,
    translated by Patrick Hanan (2009)

Cao Naiqian, *There's Nothing I Can Do When I Think of You Late at Night*, translated by
    John Balcom (2009)

Park Wan-suh, *Who Ate Up All the Shinga?* translated by Yu Young-nan and Stephen J.
    Epstein (2009)

Hwang Sun-Wŏn, *Lost Souls: Stories*, translated by Bruce and Ju-Chan Fulton (2009)

History, Society, and Culture   **CAROL GLUCK, EDITOR**

Takeuchi Yoshimi, *What Is Modernity? Writings of Takeuchi Yoshimi*, edited and
    translated, with an introduction, by Richard F. Calichman (2005)

Contemporary Japanese Thought, edited and translated by Richard F. Calichman (2005)

Overcoming Modernity, edited and translated by Richard F. Calichman (2008)

Theory of Literature *and Other Critical Writings* by Natsumi Sōseki (2009)